MATH
INSTANT ASSESSMENTS
for Data Tracking
Grade 3

Credits
Author: Erin McCarthy

Visit *carsondellosa.com* for correlations to Common Core, state, national, and Canadian provincial standards.

Carson-Dellosa Publishing, LLC
PO Box 35665
Greensboro, NC 27425 USA
carsondellosa.com

978-1-4838-3613-3
01-339161151

Table of Contents

Assessment and Data Tracking

Data tracking is an essential element in modern classrooms. Teachers are often required to capture student learning through both formative and summative assessments. They then must use the results to guide teaching, remediation, and lesson planning and provide feedback to students, parents, and administrators. Because time is always at a premium in the classroom, it is vital that teachers have the assessments they need at their fingertips. The assessments need to be suited to the skill being assessed as well as adapted to the stage in the learning process. This is true for an informal checkup at the end of a lesson or a formal assessment at the end of a unit.

This book will provide the tools and assessments needed to determine your students' level of mastery throughout the school year. The assessments are both formal and informal and include a variety of formats—pretests and posttests, flash cards, prompt cards, traditional tests, and exit tickets. Often, there are several assessment options for a single skill or concept to allow you the greatest flexibility when assessing understanding. Simply select the assessment that best fits your needs, or use them all to create a comprehensive set of assessments for before, during, and after learning.

Incorporate Instant Assessments into your daily plans to streamline the data-tracking process and keep the focus on student mastery and growth.

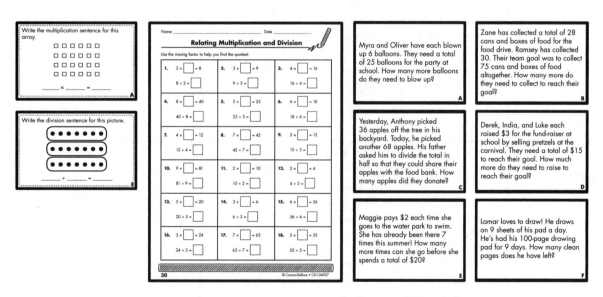

A variety of instant assessments for multiplication and division

Types of Assessment

Assessment usually has a negative association because it brings to mind tedious pencil-and-paper tests and grading. However, it can take on many different forms and be a positive, integral part of the year. Not all assessments need to be formal, nor do they all need to be graded. Choose the type of assessment to use based on the information you need to gather. Then, you can decide if or how it should be graded.

	What Does It Look Like?	Examples
Formative Assessment	• occurs during learning • is administered frequently • is usually informal and not graded • identifies areas of improvement • provides immediate feedback so a student can make adjustments promptly, if needed • allows teachers to rethink strategies, lesson content, etc., based on current student performance • is process-focused • has the most impact on a student's performance	• in-class observations • exit tickets • reflections and journaling • homework • student-teacher conferences • student self-evaluations
Interim Assessment	• occurs occasionally • is more formal and usually graded • feedback is not immediate, though still fairly quick • helps teachers identify gaps in teaching and areas for remediation • often includes performance assessments, which are individualized, authentic, and performance-based in order to evaluate higher-level thinking skills	• in-class observations • exit tickets • reflections and journaling • homework • student-teacher conferences • student self-evaluations
Summative Assessment	• occurs once learning is considered complete • the information is used by the teacher and school for broader purposes • takes time to return a grade or score • can be used to compare a student's performance to others • is product-focused • has the least impact on a student's performance since there are few or no opportunities for retesting	• cumulative projects • final portfolios • quarterly testing • end-of-the-year testing • standardized testing

How to Use This Book

The assessments in this book follow a few different formats, depending on the skill or concept being assessed. Use the descriptions below to familiarize yourself with each unique format and get the most out of Instant Assessments all year long.

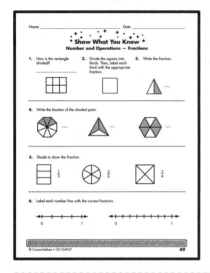

Show What You Know

Each domain begins with a pair of *Show What You Know* tests. Both tests follow the same format and include the same types of questions so they can be directly compared to show growth. Use them as a pretest and posttest. Or, use one as a test at the end of a unit and use the second version as a retest for students after remediation.

Exit Tickets

Each domain ends with exit tickets that cover the variety of concepts within the domain. Exit tickets are very targeted questions designed to assess understanding of specific skills, so they are ideal formative assessments to use at the end of a lesson. Exit tickets do not have space for student names, allowing teachers to gather information on the entire class without placing pressure on individual students. If desired, have students write their names or initials on the backs of the tickets. Other uses for exit tickets include the following:

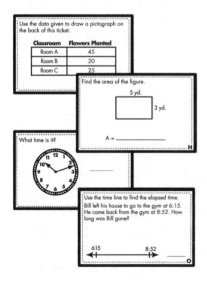

- Use the back of each ticket for longer answers, fuller explanations, or extension questions. If needed, students can staple them to larger sheets of paper.
- They can also be used for warm-ups or to find out what students know before a lesson.
- Use the generic exit tickets on pages 7 and 8 for any concept you want to assess. Be sure to fill in any blanks before copying.
- Laminate them and place them in a math center as task cards.
- Use them to play Scoot or a similar review game at the end of a unit.
- Choose several to create a targeted assessment for a skill or set of skills.

Cards

Use the cards as prompts for one-on-one conferencing. Simply copy the cards, cut them apart, and follow the directions preceding each set of cards. Use the lettering to keep track of which cards a student has interacted with.

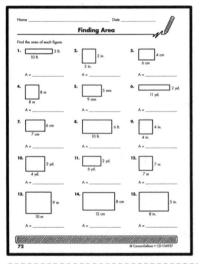

- Copy on card stock and/or laminate for durability.
- Punch holes in the top left corners and place the cards on a book ring to make them easily accessible.
- Copy the sets on different colors of paper to keep them easily separated or to distinguish different sections within a set of cards.
- Easily differentiate by using different amounts or levels of cards to assess a student.
- Write the answers on the backs of cards to create self-checking flash cards.
- Place them in a math center as task cards or matching activities.
- Use them to play Scoot or a similar review game at the end of a unit.

Assessment Pages

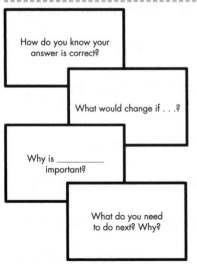

The reproducible assessment pages are intended for use as a standard test of a skill. Use them in conjunction with other types of assessment to get a full picture of a student's level of understanding. They can also be used for review or homework.

Math Talk Prompt Cards

Use the math talk prompt cards on pages 9 and 10 to prompt math discussions that can be used to informally assess students' levels of understanding. Use the math talk prompts to encourage reflection and deeper understanding of math concepts throughout the year.

- Copy on card stock and/or laminate for durability.
- Punch holes in the top left corners and place the cards on a book ring to keep them easily accessible.
- Use them for journaling prompts.
- Place them in a math center to be used with other activities.

Exit Tickets

Exit tickets are a useful formative assessment tool that you can easily work into your day. You can choose to use a single exit ticket at the end of the day or at the end of each lesson. Simply choose a ticket below and make one copy for each student. Then, have students complete the prompt and present them to you as their ticket out of the door. Use the student responses to gauge overall learning, create small remediation groups, or target areas for reteaching. A blank exit ticket is included on page 8 so you can create your own exit tickets as well.

What stuck with you today?

_____

_____

_____

_____

List three facts you learned today. Put them in order from most important to least important.

1. _____

_____

2. _____

_____

3. _____

_____

The first thing I'll tell my family about today is

_____

_____

_____

_____

_____

The most important thing I learned today is

_____

_____

_____

_____

_____

Color the face that shows how you feel about understanding today's lesson.

Explain why. _____

_____

Summarize today's lesson in 10 words or less.

_____

_____

_____

_____

One example of _____

is _____

_____

_____

_____

_____ .

One question I still have is _____

_____

_____

_____

_____

_____ .

How will understanding _____

_____

help you in real life? _____

_____

_____

_____

One new word I learned today is _____

_____ .

It means _____

_____

_____

_____ .

Draw a picture related to the lesson. Add a caption.

_____

_____

If today's lesson were a song, the title would

be _____

_____

because _____

_____

_____

The answer is _____ .

What is the question? _____

_____

_____

_____

Use these prompts when observing individual students in order to better understand their thinking and depth of understanding of a concept. These cards may also be used during whole class lessons or in small remediation groups to get students to explain their thinking with different concepts.

How did you solve it?	What strategy did you use?
How could you solve it a different way?	Can you repeat that in your own words?
Explain your thinking.	Did you use any key words? Which ones?

Can you explain why you chose to do that?	Why did you choose to add/subtract/ multiply/divide?
How do you know your answer is correct?	How can you prove your answer?
Is this like any other problems you have solved? How?	What would change if . . .?
Why is _____ important?	What do you need to do next? Why?

✦ Show What You Know ✦
Operations and Algebraic Thinking

1. Write the multiplication sentence for the array.

_____ × _____ = _____

2. Draw the array.

3 × 8

Solve.

3.
$$\begin{array}{r} 7 \\ \times\,2 \\ \hline \end{array} \qquad \begin{array}{r} 2 \\ \times\,6 \\ \hline \end{array} \qquad \begin{array}{r} 4 \\ \times\,4 \\ \hline \end{array}$$

4. $3 \times$ _____ $= 27$

$3 \times$ _____ $= 42$

5. What division problem could be solved with this array?

_____ ÷ _____ = _____

6. Draw a picture to show each problem. Then, solve.

$10 \div 2 =$ _____

$24 \div 3 =$ _____

Solve.

7. $63 \div 7 =$ _____

$45 \div 9 =$ _____

$16 \div 4 =$ _____

8. $48 \div$ _____ $= 8$

$36 \div$ _____ $= 6$

9. $8 \times 3 = 3 \times$ _____

$5 \times 4 = 4 \times$ _____

10. Solve.

$2 \times 6 \times 1 =$ _____

$7 \times 4 \times 3 =$ _____

11. Write a related multiplication or division sentence for each problem.

$30 \div 6 = 5$

_____

$40 \div 5 = 8$

_____

$7 \times 9 = 63$

_____

$3 \times 8 = 24$

_____

Solve. Show your work.

12. There are 7 girls on stage. Each girl is holding 9 flowers. How many flowers are there in all?

13. Jennifer hopped over 3 rocks. She hopped over each rock 2 times. How many times did she hop in all?

14. A pack of 42 candies is evenly divided between 7 people. How many candies does each person receive?

15. Eighteen fish were caught on a deep-sea fishing boat. If each person on the boat caught two fish, how many people were on the boat?

16. Roberto raked the leaves in his backyard. His mom paid him $3 for each bag of leaves he filled. On Friday, he filled 7 bags. On Saturday, he filled 4 bags. How much money did he make in all?

17. Patrick collects baseball cards. He has 35 cards in his collection. He buys 3 packs of 10 cards. Then, he gives his friend 4 cards. How many baseball cards does he have now?

✦ Show What You Know ✦
Operations and Algebraic Thinking

1. Write the multiplication sentence for the array.

_____ × _____ = _____

2. Draw the array.

9 × 7

Solve.

3. $6 \times 2 =$ _____

$3 \times 3 =$ _____

$8 \times 3 =$ _____

4. $5 \times$ _____ $= 50$

$12 \times$ _____ $= 36$

5. What division problem could be solved with this array?

_____ ÷ _____ = _____

6. Draw a picture to show each problem. Then, solve.

$6 \div 2 =$ _____

$15 \div 5 =$ _____

Solve.

7. $24 \div 6 =$ _____

$16 \div 2 =$ _____

$10 \div 5 =$ _____

8. $27 \div$ _____ $= 3$

_____ $\div 8 = 7$

9. $7 \times 2 = 2 \times$ _____

$4 \times 3 = 3 \times$ _____

10. Solve.

$8 \times 3 \times 2 = $ _____

$4 \times 1 \times 7 = $ _____

11. Write a related multiplication or division sentence for each problem.

$9 \times 4 = 36$

_____

$7 \times 5 = 35$

_____

$28 \div 7 = 4$

_____

$24 \div 4 = 6$

_____

Solve. Show your work.

12. Brittany had 5 bags. She placed 7 marbles in each bag. How many marbles did she have altogether?

13. The bookstore had 8 shelves in their front window. The stock boy placed 12 books on each shelf. How many books were on display in the window?

14. Alvin has 14 goldfish. He has 2 fish tanks. How many goldfish will be in each tank if he divides them evenly?

15. Dominique has 8 bracelets. She will wear the same number on each wrist. How many bracelets will she have on each wrist?

16. The Flower Club meets 2 times a week. At each meeting, the members plant 3 gardens in the community. How many gardens can the club plant over a 5-week period?

17. Jamie put 93 books on a shelf. Of the books, 21 were chapter books, 5 were picture books, and the rest were poetry books. How many books were poetry books?

Name _____ Date _____

Understanding Multiplication

Shade in an array that uses both numbers given. Write the repeated addition problem and the multiplication problem for the array.

1. 3, 4

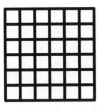

_____

_____

2. 3, 5

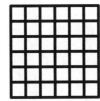

_____

_____

Shade in and label all of the arrays that can be made for each given number. Then, list all of the factors and factor pairs.

3. 15

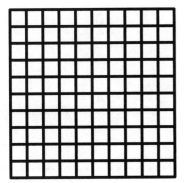

Factors: _____

Factor Pairs: _____

4. 24

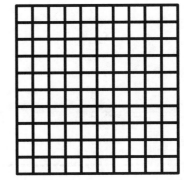

Factors: _____

Factor Pairs: _____

Draw an array for each number. Label it with the factors.

5. 36

6. 48

Multiplication Fluency

Solve.

1.
$$\begin{array}{r} 5 \\ \times\,6 \\ \hline \end{array}$$
$$\begin{array}{r} 7 \\ \times\,2 \\ \hline \end{array}$$
$$\begin{array}{r} 2 \\ \times\,6 \\ \hline \end{array}$$
$$\begin{array}{r} 4 \\ \times\,4 \\ \hline \end{array}$$
$$\begin{array}{r} 9 \\ \times\,3 \\ \hline \end{array}$$
$$\begin{array}{r} 11 \\ \times\,5 \\ \hline \end{array}$$

2.
$$\begin{array}{r} 10 \\ \times\,7 \\ \hline \end{array}$$
$$\begin{array}{r} 9 \\ \times\,7 \\ \hline \end{array}$$
$$\begin{array}{r} 10 \\ \times\,4 \\ \hline \end{array}$$
$$\begin{array}{r} 7 \\ \times\,9 \\ \hline \end{array}$$
$$\begin{array}{r} 5 \\ \times\,2 \\ \hline \end{array}$$
$$\begin{array}{r} 3 \\ \times\,4 \\ \hline \end{array}$$

3.
$$\begin{array}{r} 2 \\ \times\,9 \\ \hline \end{array}$$
$$\begin{array}{r} 3 \\ \times\,3 \\ \hline \end{array}$$
$$\begin{array}{r} 6 \\ \times\,4 \\ \hline \end{array}$$
$$\begin{array}{r} 7 \\ \times\,7 \\ \hline \end{array}$$
$$\begin{array}{r} 9 \\ \times\,8 \\ \hline \end{array}$$
$$\begin{array}{r} 5 \\ \times\,4 \\ \hline \end{array}$$

4.
$$\begin{array}{r} 9 \\ \times\,8 \\ \hline \end{array}$$
$$\begin{array}{r} 10 \\ \times\,6 \\ \hline \end{array}$$
$$\begin{array}{r} 11 \\ \times\,2 \\ \hline \end{array}$$
$$\begin{array}{r} 2 \\ \times\,4 \\ \hline \end{array}$$
$$\begin{array}{r} 3 \\ \times\,7 \\ \hline \end{array}$$
$$\begin{array}{r} 5 \\ \times\,9 \\ \hline \end{array}$$

5.
$$\begin{array}{r} 9 \\ \times\,1 \\ \hline \end{array}$$
$$\begin{array}{r} 4 \\ \times\,2 \\ \hline \end{array}$$
$$\begin{array}{r} 7 \\ \times\,3 \\ \hline \end{array}$$
$$\begin{array}{r} 4 \\ \times\,5 \\ \hline \end{array}$$
$$\begin{array}{r} 10 \\ \times\,2 \\ \hline \end{array}$$
$$\begin{array}{r} 4 \\ \times\,8 \\ \hline \end{array}$$

6.
$$\begin{array}{r} 6 \\ \times\,9 \\ \hline \end{array}$$
$$\begin{array}{r} 8 \\ \times\,3 \\ \hline \end{array}$$
$$\begin{array}{r} 7 \\ \times\,4 \\ \hline \end{array}$$
$$\begin{array}{r} 6 \\ \times\,5 \\ \hline \end{array}$$
$$\begin{array}{r} 4 \\ \times\,7 \\ \hline \end{array}$$
$$\begin{array}{r} 3 \\ \times\,7 \\ \hline \end{array}$$

7.
$$\begin{array}{r} 10 \\ \times\,1 \\ \hline \end{array}$$
$$\begin{array}{r} 2 \\ \times\,8 \\ \hline \end{array}$$
$$\begin{array}{r} 7 \\ \times\,5 \\ \hline \end{array}$$
$$\begin{array}{r} 8 \\ \times\,6 \\ \hline \end{array}$$
$$\begin{array}{r} 8 \\ \times\,8 \\ \hline \end{array}$$
$$\begin{array}{r} 11 \\ \times\,9 \\ \hline \end{array}$$

8.
$$\begin{array}{r} 4 \\ \times\,1 \\ \hline \end{array}$$
$$\begin{array}{r} 6 \\ \times\,8 \\ \hline \end{array}$$
$$\begin{array}{r} 8 \\ \times\,9 \\ \hline \end{array}$$
$$\begin{array}{r} 9 \\ \times\,4 \\ \hline \end{array}$$
$$\begin{array}{r} 6 \\ \times\,1 \\ \hline \end{array}$$
$$\begin{array}{r} 8 \\ \times\,7 \\ \hline \end{array}$$

9.
$$\begin{array}{r} 5 \\ \times\,5 \\ \hline \end{array}$$
$$\begin{array}{r} 6 \\ \times\,3 \\ \hline \end{array}$$
$$\begin{array}{r} 8 \\ \times\,4 \\ \hline \end{array}$$
$$\begin{array}{r} 3 \\ \times\,8 \\ \hline \end{array}$$
$$\begin{array}{r} 5 \\ \times\,8 \\ \hline \end{array}$$
$$\begin{array}{r} 9 \\ \times\,9 \\ \hline \end{array}$$

Multiplication Fluency

Solve.

1.
$$\begin{array}{r}3\\\times 9\\\hline\end{array}\qquad\begin{array}{r}7\\\times 6\\\hline\end{array}\qquad\begin{array}{r}5\\\times 4\\\hline\end{array}\qquad\begin{array}{r}7\\\times 9\\\hline\end{array}\qquad\begin{array}{r}8\\\times 6\\\hline\end{array}\qquad\begin{array}{r}5\\\times 0\\\hline\end{array}$$

2.
$$\begin{array}{r}4\\\times 3\\\hline\end{array}\qquad\begin{array}{r}8\\\times 5\\\hline\end{array}\qquad\begin{array}{r}4\\\times 9\\\hline\end{array}\qquad\begin{array}{r}3\\\times 0\\\hline\end{array}\qquad\begin{array}{r}5\\\times 7\\\hline\end{array}\qquad\begin{array}{r}2\\\times 9\\\hline\end{array}$$

3.
$$\begin{array}{r}5\\\times 1\\\hline\end{array}\qquad\begin{array}{r}4\\\times 6\\\hline\end{array}\qquad\begin{array}{r}8\\\times 2\\\hline\end{array}\qquad\begin{array}{r}6\\\times 8\\\hline\end{array}\qquad\begin{array}{r}4\\\times 0\\\hline\end{array}\qquad\begin{array}{r}11\\\times 3\\\hline\end{array}$$

4.
$$\begin{array}{r}3\\\times 1\\\hline\end{array}\qquad\begin{array}{r}12\\\times 5\\\hline\end{array}\qquad\begin{array}{r}6\\\times 4\\\hline\end{array}\qquad\begin{array}{r}9\\\times 2\\\hline\end{array}\qquad\begin{array}{r}3\\\times 4\\\hline\end{array}\qquad\begin{array}{r}6\\\times 3\\\hline\end{array}$$

5.
$$\begin{array}{r}3\\\times 8\\\hline\end{array}\qquad\begin{array}{r}10\\\times 5\\\hline\end{array}\qquad\begin{array}{r}3\\\times 6\\\hline\end{array}\qquad\begin{array}{r}7\\\times 6\\\hline\end{array}\qquad\begin{array}{r}9\\\times 9\\\hline\end{array}\qquad\begin{array}{r}8\\\times 4\\\hline\end{array}$$

6.
$$\begin{array}{r}2\\\times 6\\\hline\end{array}\qquad\begin{array}{r}12\\\times 4\\\hline\end{array}\qquad\begin{array}{r}8\\\times 8\\\hline\end{array}\qquad\begin{array}{r}9\\\times 3\\\hline\end{array}\qquad\begin{array}{r}7\\\times 4\\\hline\end{array}\qquad\begin{array}{r}8\\\times 0\\\hline\end{array}$$

7.
$$\begin{array}{r}7\\\times 7\\\hline\end{array}\qquad\begin{array}{r}9\\\times 2\\\hline\end{array}\qquad\begin{array}{r}12\\\times 2\\\hline\end{array}\qquad\begin{array}{r}8\\\times 5\\\hline\end{array}\qquad\begin{array}{r}5\\\times 8\\\hline\end{array}\qquad\begin{array}{r}2\\\times 9\\\hline\end{array}$$

8.
$$\begin{array}{r}11\\\times 7\\\hline\end{array}\qquad\begin{array}{r}4\\\times 6\\\hline\end{array}\qquad\begin{array}{r}7\\\times 3\\\hline\end{array}\qquad\begin{array}{r}6\\\times 1\\\hline\end{array}\qquad\begin{array}{r}7\\\times 2\\\hline\end{array}\qquad\begin{array}{r}3\\\times 5\\\hline\end{array}$$

9.
$$\begin{array}{r}10\\\times 9\\\hline\end{array}\qquad\begin{array}{r}6\\\times 2\\\hline\end{array}\qquad\begin{array}{r}5\\\times 5\\\hline\end{array}\qquad\begin{array}{r}9\\\times 1\\\hline\end{array}\qquad\begin{array}{r}2\\\times 4\\\hline\end{array}\qquad\begin{array}{r}3\\\times 7\\\hline\end{array}$$

Unknowns in Multiplication

Circle the correct answer in each box.

1. _____ × 4 = 12 Trent says 3. Kayla says 8.	**2.** 24 = _____ × 4 Trent says 6. Kayla says 12.
3. 12 = _____ × 4 Trent says 3. Kayla says 5.	**4.** 7 × _____ = 56 Trent says 9. Kayla says 8.
5. _____ × 5 = 45 Trent says 4. Kayla says 9.	**6.** 8 = _____ × 4 Trent says 2. Kayla says 4.
7. 6 × _____ = 12 Trent says 12. Kayla says 2.	**8.** 20 = 10 × _____ Trent says 200. Kayla says 2.
9. 9 × _____ = 90 Trent says 11. Kayla says 10.	**10.** 4 = _____ × 2 Trent says 2. Kayla says 4.
11. _____ × 9 = 36 Trent says 4. Kayla says 3.	**12.** 9 × _____ = 45 Trent says 9. Kayla says 5.
13. 6 × _____ = 30 Trent says 5. Kayla says 24.	**14.** 36 = _____ × 6 Trent says 20. Kayla says 6.
15. _____ × 5 = 10 Trent says 2. Kayla says 50.	**16.** 72 = _____ × 6 Trent says 9. Kayla says 12.

Name _____ Date _____

Understanding Division

Write the missing numbers.

1.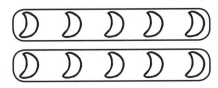

_____ ÷ _____ = _____

2.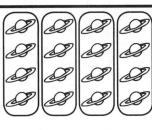

_____ ÷ _____ = _____

Circle equal groups to find the quotient.

3.

ⓒ ⓒ ⓒ ⓒ ⓒ ⓒ
ⓒ ⓒ ⓒ ⓒ ⓒ ⓒ
ⓒ ⓒ ⓒ ⓒ ⓒ ⓒ

18 ÷ 3 = _____

4.

□ □ □ □ □
□ □ □ □ □
□ □ □ □ □
□ □ □ □ □

20 ÷ 5 = _____

Draw a picture to match the division problem. Then, write the equation. Solve.

5. twelve divided into three sets

_____ ÷ _____ = _____

6. five divided into one set

_____ ÷ _____ = _____

7. twelve divided into four sets

_____ ÷ _____ = _____

8. eighteen divided into six sets

_____ ÷ _____ = _____

Division Fluency

Solve.

1. $5\overline{)30}$ $4\overline{)36}$ $2\overline{)18}$ $4\overline{)16}$ $3\overline{)27}$ $9\overline{)9}$

2. $3\overline{)24}$ $4\overline{)32}$ $3\overline{)9}$ $8\overline{)56}$ $9\overline{)36}$ $6\overline{)18}$

3. $8\overline{)64}$ $9\overline{)81}$ $7\overline{)28}$ $7\overline{)49}$ $8\overline{)16}$ $1\overline{)4}$

4. $8\overline{)40}$ $9\overline{)18}$ $6\overline{)48}$ $6\overline{)54}$ $7\overline{)56}$ $4\overline{)28}$

5. $3\overline{)30}$ $2\overline{)14}$ $8\overline{)48}$ $5\overline{)45}$ $4\overline{)20}$ $9\overline{)63}$

6. $5\overline{)15}$ $1\overline{)9}$ $3\overline{)6}$ $8\overline{)72}$ $6\overline{)24}$ $6\overline{)36}$

7. $8\overline{)32}$ $4\overline{)12}$ $8\overline{)24}$ $7\overline{)14}$ $2\overline{)20}$ $8\overline{)8}$

Division Fluency

Solve.

1. $5 \overline{)25}$ $4 \overline{)16}$ $7 \overline{)21}$ $9 \overline{)81}$ $6 \overline{)18}$ $6 \overline{)54}$

2. $3 \overline{)27}$ $9 \overline{)72}$ $7 \overline{)49}$ $5 \overline{)5}$ $3 \overline{)24}$ $4 \overline{)28}$

3. $9 \overline{)36}$ $2 \overline{)14}$ $1 \overline{)9}$ $3 \overline{)6}$ $8 \overline{)16}$ $7 \overline{)35}$

4. $5 \overline{)15}$ $3 \overline{)9}$ $7 \overline{)42}$ $9 \overline{)45}$ $2 \overline{)2}$ $7 \overline{)63}$

5. $2 \overline{)6}$ $5 \overline{)20}$ $2 \overline{)18}$ $8 \overline{)32}$ $4 \overline{)24}$ $8 \overline{)72}$

6. $1 \overline{)1}$ $8 \overline{)64}$ $6 \overline{)36}$ $5 \overline{)45}$ $2 \overline{)16}$ $8 \overline{)48}$

7. $3 \overline{)15}$ $3 \overline{)21}$ $9 \overline{)54}$ $1 \overline{)5}$ $8 \overline{)24}$ $7 \overline{)28}$

Unknowns in Division

Circle the correct answer in each box.

1. $6 \div$ _____ $= 3$ Blair says 3. Evan says 2.	**2.** _____ $\div 9 = 3$ Blair says 18. Evan says 27.
3. $36 \div 4 =$ _____ Blair says 6. Evan says 9.	**4.** $54 \div$ _____ $= 6$ Blair says 5. Evan says 9.
5. _____ $\div 2 = 12$ Blair says 24. Evan says 10.	**6.** $8 =$ _____ $\times 4$ Blair says 2. Evan says 4.
7. $40 \div 8 =$ _____ Blair says 6. Evan says 5.	**8.** _____ $\div 3 = 6$ Blair says 19. Evan says 18.
9. $6 \div$ _____ $= 2$ Blair says 5. Evan says 3.	**10.** $9 \div$ _____ $= 3$ Blair says 1. Evan says 3.
11. $16 \div 2 =$ _____ Blair says 8. Evan says 4.	**12.** $20 \div 2 =$ _____ Blair says 11. Evan says 10.
13. _____ $\div 4 = 8$ Blair says 32. Evan says 34.	**14.** $27 \div$ _____ $= 9$ Blair says 3. Evan says 2.
15. $8 \div$ _____ $= 2$ Blair says 4. Evan says 6.	**16.** $24 \div 6 =$ _____ Blair says 6. Evan says 4.

Multiplication and Division
Word Problems

Present a student with a word problem card to assess their proficiency with solving word problems. Or, choose several to create a whole-class assessment. You can assess how a student interprets word problems by giving her several cards, having her sort them by the operation needed, and asking her to explain her reasoning. If desired, laminate the cards so students can use write-on/wipe-away markers to identify key words and numbers. Word problems are separated into one-step multiplication problems (cards A–R) and one-step division problems (S–AL), and contain unknowns in all positions.

Sara has 10 flowers. Each one has 7 petals. How many petals are there in all?

A

If a cyclist travels 12 miles per hour, how far can she travel in 4 hours?

B

Forrest is coloring eggs. Each container holds 12 eggs. Forrest has 5 containers of colors. How many eggs will Forrest color?

C

We looked under 7 rocks. Each rock had 2 snails underneath it. How many snails did we see?

D

On the beach are 8 towels. On each towel are 6 buckets. How many buckets are there in all?

E

April found 9 seashells. Each shell had an animal living in it. How many animals did April find?

F

Drew invited 5 friends to his party. He wants to give each person 4 stickers. How many stickers will he need?

G

Our class ate 8 pizzas. Each pizza had 12 slices. How many slices did we eat in all?

H

Isabella's 4 guinea pigs each ate 8 seeds. How many seeds did they eat in all?

I

Jason is making lemonade for 10 people. Each glass needs 3 spoons of mix. How many spoons of lemonade mix will Jason use?

J

Norman ate 6 strawberries each day for a week. How many strawberries did Norman eat in all?

K

Tyrone and 3 of his friends went to get ice cream. Each person got 3 scoops of ice cream. How many scoops did they eat in all?

L

Mark found 7 spiderwebs. Each web had trapped 5 bugs. How many bugs were trapped in all?

M

Penny had 12 nickels. How much money did she have?

N

Sasha collected flowers. She put them in 9 vases. She put 8 flowers in each vase. How many flowers did she collect in all?

O

Ruby visited the library on Wednesday, Thursday, and Friday. On each day, she read 5 short stories. How many stories did Ruby read in all?

P

The zookeeper gave 2 bags of peanuts to an elephant. There were 12 peanuts in each bag. How many peanuts did the zookeeper give to the elephant?

Q

Pablo wants to play flag football with 9 of his friends. Each player needs 2 flags. How many flags are needed so that all 9 friends and Pablo can play flag football together?

R

Mr. Lang passes out 24 papers equally to 8 students. How many papers does each child get?

S

Avery and Vanessa share 12 cookies evenly. How many cookies does each girl get?

T

Erica collected 63 shells each morning during the week she stayed at the beach. She collected the same amount each morning. How many shells did she collect each morning?

U

Brady has 28 grapes. He wants to put them in bags for lunch for the next 4 days. How many grapes should he put in each bag if he wants the same amount each day?

V

A box contains 42 dog treats. Felicia divides them evenly and gives 7 treats to each of her dogs. How many dogs does Felicia have?

W

Lucy sewed 4 buttons on each doll she made. She used 32 buttons in all. How many dolls did Lucy make?

X

Jake has to put 72 erasers into 8 boxes. How many erasers should go in each box if he wants an equal amount in each box?

Y

A group of 3 friends are splitting a package of 24 pencils. How many pencils should each person get?

Z

Grandma's famous cake recipe calls for 2 eggs. Grandma has a dozen eggs. How many cakes can she bake?

AA

Mrs. Pappas had 40 books. She gave 8 books to each group of students. How many groups were there?

AB

Gavin had 56 bugs in his collection. He has 8 of each type of bug. How many different types of bugs are in Gavin's collection?

AC

Jeff had 36 bags of popcorn to sell. He sold all of the popcorn to 6 customers. If each customer bought the same amount, how many bags did each customer buy?

AD

Lauren is making 5 pizzas. She has 25 pepperoni slices to divide between the pizzas. How many pepperoni slices should go on each pizza?

AE

A family of 5 takes an ice chest with 10 water bottles in it to the beach. How many water bottles will each person receive if the water bottles are divided evenly?

AF

Sally has 24 shoes in her closet. A pair of shoes is a matched set of 2 shoes. How many pairs of shoes does Sally have?

AG

There are 12 months in a year. There are 4 seasons in a year. If each season has an equal number of months, how many months make up each season?

AH

Mrs. Robinson ordered 63 tables and 7 chairs for a banquet. Each table will have the same number of chairs. How many chairs will be at each table?

AI

Mr. Walsh has 18 books to place on 3 shelves. He wants to put the same number of books on each shelf. How many books should he put on each shelf?

AJ

Riley earned $27 for mowing 3 lawns. Riley earned the same amount of money for each lawn. How much did he earn for each lawn?

AK

In the pasture there are 88 horse legs. How many horses are there?

AL

Multistep Word Problems

Present a student with a multistep word problem card to assess their proficiency with solving multistep word problems. Or, choose several to create a whole-class assessment. You can assess how a student interprets word problems by giving him several cards and asking him to identify the operations needed for each problem or explain how many steps he had to take to get to the correct answer. If desired, laminate the cards so that students can use write-on/wipe away markers to identify key words and numbers.

Myra and Oliver have each blown up 6 balloons. They need a total of 25 balloons for the party at school. How many more balloons do they need to blow up?

A

Zane has collected a total of 28 cans and boxes of food for the food drive. Ramsey has collected 30. Their team goal was to collect 75 cans and boxes of food altogether. How many more do they need to collect to reach their goal?

B

Yesterday, Anthony picked 36 apples off the tree in his backyard. Today, he picked another 68 apples. His father asked him to divide the total in half so that they could share their apples with the food bank. How many apples did they donate?

C

Derek, India, and Luke each raised $3 for the fund-raiser at school by selling pretzels at the carnival. They need a total of $15 to reach their goal. How much more do they need to raise to reach their goal?

D

Maggie pays $2 each time she goes to the water park to swim. She has already been there 7 times this summer! How many more times can she go before she spends a total of $20?

E

Lamar loves to draw! He draws on 9 sheets of his pad a day. He's had his 100-page drawing pad for 9 days. How many clean pages does he have left?

F

Mario has 4 nickels in each of his 3 pockets. How much money does Mario have?

G

Five bags each hold eight marbles. Ten of the marbles rolled under the table. How many marbles are left?

H

Six bags each hold seven fruit snacks. Three snacks were eaten. Are there are enough left to share equally with three people? Explain.

I

Nicole used 342 beads to make a bracelet. She used 813 beads to make a necklace. If the package started with 1,500 beads, how many beads are left?

J

Shelby practiced free throws. On 4 days she made 8 shots each day. On 3 days, she made 9 shots each day. How many shots did she make all week?

K

Seven words each have 2 vowels and 5 consonants. How many letters are there in the 7 words? How many vowels? Consonants?

L

Eight cups are on the table. Each cup needs 10 gumdrops in it. One bag has 50 gumdrops in it. Is one bag enough to fill the 8 cups? Explain.

M

Sarah found 31 flowers in her backyard. She found 29 more in her friend's yard. She divided the flowers equally between 5 vases. How many flowers did she put in each vase?

N

Name _____ Date _____

Multiplication and Division
Word Problems

Solve.

1. Bailey wants to buy 6 pieces of bubble gum. Each piece costs 5 cents. How much will she have to pay for the bubble gum?	**2.** A swimming pool has 20 swimmers. An equal number of swimmers are in the deep end and in the shallow end of the pool. How many swimmers are in each end of the pool?
3. The PE teacher has 6 balls to give 6 teams. How many balls did the teacher give to each team?	**4.** There are 9 rows of 9 computers. How many computers are in the office altogether?
5. Brianna buys 7 boxes of Gingersnap Delights. Each box has 9 cookies. How many Gingersnap Delights does she have in all?	**6.** Hamilton tackled a total of 42 football players in the last 6 games. He tackled the same number of players each game. How many players did Hamilton tackle during each game?

Relating Multiplication and Division

Use the missing factor to help you find the quotient. Write each missing number.

1. $2 \times \boxed{} = 8$

$8 \div 2 = \boxed{}$

2. $3 \times \boxed{} = 9$

$9 \div 3 = \boxed{}$

3. $4 \times \boxed{} = 16$

$16 \div 4 = \boxed{}$

4. $8 \times \boxed{} = 40$

$40 \div 8 = \boxed{}$

5. $5 \times \boxed{} = 25$

$25 \div 5 = \boxed{}$

6. $6 \times \boxed{} = 18$

$18 \div 6 = \boxed{}$

7. $4 \times \boxed{} = 12$

$12 \div 4 = \boxed{}$

8. $7 \times \boxed{} = 42$

$42 \div 7 = \boxed{}$

9. $3 \times \boxed{} = 15$

$15 \div 3 = \boxed{}$

10. $9 \times \boxed{} = 81$

$81 \div 9 = \boxed{}$

11. $2 \times \boxed{} = 10$

$10 \div 2 = \boxed{}$

12. $2 \times \boxed{} = 4$

$4 \div 2 = \boxed{}$

13. $5 \times \boxed{} = 20$

$20 \div 5 = \boxed{}$

14. $3 \times \boxed{} = 6$

$6 \div 3 = \boxed{}$

15. $6 \times \boxed{} = 36$

$36 \div 6 = \boxed{}$

16. $3 \times \boxed{} = 24$

$24 \div 3 = \boxed{}$

17. $7 \times \boxed{} = 63$

$63 \div 7 = \boxed{}$

18. $5 \times \boxed{} = 55$

$55 \div 5 = \boxed{}$

Write the multiplication sentence for this array.

□ □ □ □ □ □
□ □ □ □ □ □
□ □ □ □ □ □
□ □ □ □ □ □

_____ × _____ = _____

A

Draw the array for this multiplication sentence.

6 × 8

B

Solve.

1. 5 × 4 = _____   **2.** 3 × 6 = _____

3. 7 × 2 = _____   **4.** 6 × 9 = _____

5. 3 × 10 = _____   **6.** 4 × 6 = _____

7. 2 × 8 = _____   **8.** 12 × 2 = _____

C

Write the number that makes each equation true.

1. 5 × _____ = 45   **2.** _____ × 9 = 72

3. _____ × 6 = 30   **4.** 4 × _____ = 32

5. 8 ÷ 2 = _____   **6.** 24 ÷ 2 = _____

7. 36 ÷ 4 = _____   **8.** 15 ÷ _____ = 3

D

Write the division sentence for this picture.

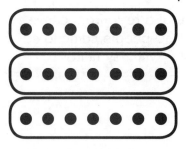

_____ ÷ _____ = _____

E

Draw the arrays for the number sentences given. Then, solve.

12 ÷ 4 = _____   18 ÷ 2 = _____

F

Solve.

1. 49 ÷ 7 = _____   **2.** 30 ÷ 5 = _____

3. 21 ÷ 3 = _____   **4.** 24 ÷ 8 = _____

5. 44 ÷ 4 = _____   **6.** 48 ÷ 6 = _____

7. 28 ÷ 7 = _____   **8.** 12 ÷ 3 = _____

G

Write a related multiplication or division sentence for each problem.

1. 27 ÷ 9 = 3 _____

2. 9 × 2 = 18 _____

3. 10 × 5 = 50 _____

4. 56 ÷ 8 = 7 _____

H

Solve.

A clown had 11 balloons that he sold at a carnival for 6 cents each. If he sold all 11 balloons, how much money did he make?

I

Solve.

The movie rental store charges $1 to rent each movie. Ms. Lopez rents 6 movies. How much will the movie rental store charge her?

J

Solve.

Carrie runs 7 miles, 4 times a week. How many miles does she run in one week?

K

Solve.

Hayden has 14 pieces of gum. He shares the gum equally with his sister. How many pieces of gum do they each get?

L

Solve.

A group of 4 friends shared 36 counters equally. How many counters did each friend get?

M

Solve.

Each table at a restaurant can seat 6 people. A party of 30 people came to eat. How many tables will they need?

N

Solve.

Our family drove 642 miles on vacation. We crossed 5 states. We stopped 3 times in 4 states and 2 times in the last state. How many times did we stop in all?

O

Solve.

Hunter's goal is to find 1,000 insects. In one park, he counted 268 bugs. In another park, he counted 521 bugs. How many more insects does he need to find to reach his goal?

P

Name _____ Date _____

Number and Operations in Base Ten

Solve.

1. 239
   + 293

2. 857
   − 675

3. 955
   + 134

4. 725
   − 469

5. 627
   − 469

6. 478
   + 655

7. 784
   − 591

8. 456
   + 327

9. 434
   + 948

10. 423
    − 155

11. 831
    − 357

12. 940
    − 556

13. 824
    − 548

14. 349
    + 233

15. 574
    − 293

16. 438
    − 254

17. 588
    + 294

18. 825
    − 638

19. 945
    + 379

20. 748
    − 353

21. Solve.

$$\begin{array}{r} 10 \\ 6 \\ + 8 \\ \hline \end{array} \qquad \begin{array}{r} 22 \\ 86 \\ + 34 \\ \hline \end{array} \qquad \begin{array}{r} 67 \\ 35 \\ + 18 \\ \hline \end{array}$$

- -

22. Round to the nearest 10.

72 _____   83 _____   49 _____   55 _____

17 _____   34 _____   62 _____   95 _____

- -

23. Round to the nearest 100.

728 _____   438 _____   284 _____   192 _____

561 _____   924 _____   689 _____   54 _____

- -

Solve.

24. There are 990 seats in the stadium. If there are 587 people in the stadium, how many empty seats are there?

25. At the basketball game, 232 adult tickets were sold and 179 children's tickets were sold. How many tickets were sold for the basketball game?

26. The shoe store has 324 pairs of athletic shoes and 187 pairs of sandals. How many pairs of athletic shoes and sandals does the shoe store have in all?

- -

27. Solve.

$$\begin{array}{r} 30 \\ \times 3 \\ \hline \end{array} \quad \begin{array}{r} 40 \\ \times 4 \\ \hline \end{array} \quad \begin{array}{r} 50 \\ \times 8 \\ \hline \end{array} \quad \begin{array}{r} 90 \\ \times 6 \\ \hline \end{array} \quad \begin{array}{r} 60 \\ \times 4 \\ \hline \end{array} \quad \begin{array}{r} 80 \\ \times 2 \\ \hline \end{array} \quad \begin{array}{r} 60 \\ \times 8 \\ \hline \end{array}$$

Name _____   Date _____

✦ Show What You Know ✦
Number and Operations in Base Ten

Solve.

1.   979
        + 654

2.   870
        + 739

3.   675
        + 597

4.   654
        − 265

5.   531
        − 174

6.   293
        − 187

7.   845
        − 566

8.   827
        − 529

9.   638
        + 422

10.   539
        + 468

11.   536
        − 258

12.   667
        + 291

13.   646
        + 668

14.   348
        + 489

15.   487
        − 391

16.   485
        + 159

17.   648
        + 437

18.   890
        − 249

19.   496
        − 288

20.   392
        + 389

21. Solve.

19	62	90
17	35	20
+ 8	+ 23	+ 10

---

22. Round to the nearest 10.

63 _____   92 _____   58 _____   64 _____

28 _____   45 _____   71 _____   84 _____

---

23. Round to the nearest 100.

364 _____   886 _____   863 _____   713 _____

543 _____   765 _____   451 _____   123 _____

Solve.

24. Ben earned $135 during his first week of work. He earned $213 during his second week of work. How much money did Ben earn during the two weeks of work?

25. In the year 1998, an antique vase was 239 years old. In what year was the vase made?

26. Mr. Silva had $539 in his savings account. He withdrew $259. How much money does Mr. Silva have left?

---

27. Solve.

10	20	30	40	60	40	30
× 3	× 3	× 3	× 5	× 2	× 3	× 2

Adding and Subtracting
up to 3-Digit Numbers

Solve each problem. Regroup when necessary.

1. 634
    + 268

2. 987
    + 89

3. 768
    − 479

4. 888
    + 276

5. 747
    − 458

6. 950
    − 580

7. 562
    + 123

8. 321
    − 109

9. 982
    + 171

10. 745
    − 152

11. 782
    + 41

12. 830
    − 710

13. 301
    − 242

14. 349
    + 33

15. 878
    + 287

16. 727
    − 49

17. 948
    + 348

18. 847
    − 358

19. 312
    + 123

20. 626
    − 146

21. 975
    + 681

22. 457
    − 309

23. 862
    + 313

24. 729
    − 21

25. 703
    − 78

26. 653
    + 307

27. 584
    − 295

28. 600
    − 367

29. 298
    + 113

30. 393
    + 298

Adding Three Numbers

Solve each problem. Regroup when necessary.

1. 9 6 + 4	**2.** 7 6 + 8	**3.** 14 11 + 5	**4.** 19 17 + 8	**5.** 53 32 + 12	**6.** 8 6 + 2

1.   9
    6
 + 4

2.   7
    6
 + 8

3. 14
   11
 + 5

4. 19
   17
 + 8

5. 53
   32
 + 12

6.   8
    6
 + 2

7. 17
   93
 + 23

8. 16
   45
 + 92

9. 82
   18
 + 23

10. 57
   19
 + 7

11. 22
   86
 + 34

12. 50
   40
 + 60

13. 86
   93
 + 72

14. 23
   35
 + 62

15. 67
   35
 + 18

16. 86
   54
 + 83

17. 32
   49
 + 76

18. 60
   25
 + 10

19. 25
   66
 + 72

20. 81
   19
 + 83

21. 53
   42
 + 93

22. 13
   12
 + 14

23. 90
   20
 + 10

24. 82
   76
 + 54

25. 86
   54
 + 32

26. 92
   10
 + 53

27. 81
   71
 + 36

28. 12
   18
 + 24

29. 93
   48
 + 13

30. 41
   86
 + 53

31. 22
   67
 + 51

32. 68
   21
 + 45

33. 15
   20
 + 30

34. 62
   32
 + 11

35. 29
   18
 + 67

36. 83
   21
 + 23

Name _____   Date _____

Relating Addition and Subtraction

Add or subtract. Check each answer. Show your work.

1. 212
      + 157

2. 719
      + 182

3. 321
      – 83

4. 312
      + 105

5. 125
      – 92

6. 983
      – 657

7. 519
      + 213

8. 456
      – 291

9. 442
      – 220

10. 306
       + 215

11. 170
       + 120

12. 442
       – 220

13. 300
       – 179

14. 119
       – 104

15. 710
       + 398

16. 423
       – 197

17. 357
       + 249

18. 712
       + 291

19. 259
       – 147

20. 592
       – 463

21. 714
       + 291

22. 312
       + 85

23. 708
       – 412

24. 419
       + 57

Name _____ Date _____

Adding and Subtracting
up to 4-Digit Numbers

Solve each problem. Regroup when necessary.

1. 5,120 + 1,436	**2.** 5,190 + 4,125	**3.** 5,032 + 1,764	**4.** 4,321 + 2,841	**5.** 5,960 + 4,011
6. 1,340 – 380	**7.** 1,960 – 420	**8.** 2,720 – 340	**9.** 5,120 – 1,780	**10.** 4,963 – 1,082
11. 5,947 + 272	**12.** 5,803 – 993	**13.** 1,906 – 1,173	**14.** 1,876 + 759	**15.** 4,120 – 3,290
16. 1,982 + 1,782	**17.** 7,083 + 2,907	**18.** 4,325 + 4,986	**19.** 6,057 + 1,239	**20.** 8,761 + 1,032
21. 6,932 – 2,840	**22.** 1,389 – 794	**23.** 2,545 – 963	**24.** 7,863 – 2,572	**25.** 8,121 – 640
26. 9,876 – 985	**27.** 3,981 + 1,543	**28.** 7,121 + 1,923	**29.** 8,160 – 4,670	**30.** 7,805 – 164

Addition and Subtraction
Word Problems

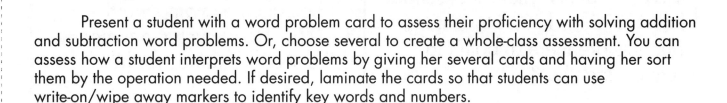

Present a student with a word problem card to assess their proficiency with solving addition and subtraction word problems. Or, choose several to create a whole-class assessment. You can assess how a student interprets word problems by giving her several cards and having her sort them by the operation needed. If desired, laminate the cards so that students can use write-on/wipe away markers to identify key words and numbers.

There are 119 houses on Green Street. The postal carrier has only 57 flyers to deliver to Green Street. How many more flyers does he need? **A**	At the local elementary school, there are 543 boys and 476 girls. How many total students are there? **B**
Ms. Lewis has 639 red tiles and 722 blue tiles. How many red and blue tiles does Ms. Lewis have? **C**	A bicycle costs $530. There is a rebate for $147. How much will the bike cost after the rebate? **D**
There were 700 purple and yellow paper clips in the package. If 190 of the paper clips were yellow, how many paper clips were purple? **E**	Ivy has 519 pennies. Jordana has 542 pennies. How many pennies do they have altogether? **F**

A local high school has 1,523 students. Their rival school has 1,695 students. How many students are there at both high schools together?

G

Logan has a stamp worth $1,050. He has another stamp worth $1,072. How much more money is the second stamp worth?

H

In the year 1996, Mr. Westberg's car was considered a classic. The car was made in 1942. How old was Mr. Westberg's car in 1996?

I

Krystal read 534 pages last week and 352 pages this week. How many pages did Krystal read altogether?

J

Lola bought a roll of cloth that was 197 inches long. She cut 85 inches off the roll to use in a project. How many inches did she have left on the roll?

K

Mr. Edwards is 43 years old. Mrs. Gladd is 52 years old. Ms. Kaplan is 39 years old. What is their combined age?

L

Andrew bought three boards at the home center. The boards are 86, 32, and 19 inches long. What is the combined length of the three boards?

M

Bonnie wants to visit her grandmother who lives 2,583 miles away. The airplane will only take her 2,392 miles toward her destination. Bonnie needs to rent a car to drive the remaining miles. How many miles does Bonnie need to drive?

N

Rounding Numbers

Round to the nearest 10.

1. 45 _____   95 _____   81 _____   28 _____   53 _____

2. 33 _____   67 _____   49 _____   17 _____   15 _____

3. 98 _____   12 _____   59 _____   51 _____   37 _____

Round to the nearest 100.

4. 710 _____   250 _____   134 _____   827 _____   359 _____

5. 744 _____   244 _____   411 _____   456 _____   278 _____

6. 904 _____   530 _____   862 _____   761 _____   547 _____

Round to the underlined place value.

7. 2,714 _____   8,041 _____   9,687 _____   3,327 _____

8. 2,835 _____   4,698 _____   3,896 _____   9,559 _____

9. 236 _____   291 _____   3,212 _____   2,567 _____

10. 5,671 _____   7,779 _____   4,221 _____   6,555 _____

Multiplying by Multiples of 10

Solve.

1.   60
    × 9

2.   30
    × 7

3.   80
    × 8

4.   60
    × 8

5.   60
    × 5

6.   50
    × 8

7.   90
    × 9

8.   50
    × 3

9.   90
    × 2

10.   20
     × 6

11.   70
     × 6

12.   80
     × 6

13.   20
     × 9

14.   30
     × 8

15.   70
     × 4

16.   50
     × 7

17.   70
     × 2

18.   20
     × 5

19.   70
     × 7

20.   90
     × 5

Solve.

710 − 498	697 − 561	963 + 255
599 − 495	833 − 804	641 + 99

A

Add.

36 6 + 7	53 87 + 66	42 76 + 6	96 15 + 41

B

Add.

71 11 + 88	61 12 + 9	30 5 + 7	34 68 + 8

C

Solve. Check each answer.

923 − 370	839 + 70

D

Solve.

1,860 − 870	2,786 + 436	2,700 + 580	7,520 − 1,800

E

Solve.

6,104 − 1,109	425 + 502	7,290 − 5,265	1,814 − 939

F

Solve.

On Monday, Sarah read 24 pages of her book. On Tuesday night, she read 41 pages, and Wednesday night, she read 32 pages. How many pages did Sarah read altogether?

G

Solve.

Patrick bought a bag of mixed nuts. There are 500 total nuts. If 345 of the nuts are peanuts, how many nuts are not peanuts?

H

Solve.

Lake Erie is 241 miles long. Lake Ontario is 193 miles long. How many miles long are Lake Erie and Lake Ontario in all?

I

Solve.

Brooke has a dog-walking business. She walked 12 dogs on Thursday, 15 dogs on Saturday, and 9 dogs on Sunday. How many dogs did Brooke walk altogether?

J

Solve.

Janelle has saved $329. If she spends $58, how much money will she have left?

K

Solve.

Greg read 320 pages in a book. Holly read 569 pages in a book. How many pages did Greg and Holly read altogether?

L

Round to the nearest 10.

67 _____	65 _____
89 _____	93 _____
52 _____	66 _____
38 _____	79 _____

M

Round to the nearest 100.

163 _____	486 _____
691 _____	207 _____
159 _____	861 _____
489 _____	892 _____

N

Round to the underlined digit.

2,334 _____	873 _____
9,319 _____	1,908 _____
3,607 _____	2,902 _____
746 _____	476 _____

O

Solve.

$$\begin{array}{ccccc} 30 & 50 & 20 & 60 & 70 \\ \times\ 5 & \times\ 2 & \times\ 3 & \times\ 5 & \times\ 4 \end{array}$$

$$\begin{array}{ccccc} 80 & 60 & 60 & 30 & 30 \\ \times\ 4 & \times\ 8 & \times\ 2 & \times\ 3 & \times\ 6 \end{array}$$

P

Show What You Know
Number and Operations—Fractions

1. How is the circle divided?

_____

2. Divide the circle into fourths. Then, label each fourth with the appropriate fraction.

3. Write the fraction.

 ___

---

4. Write the fraction of the shaded parts.

 ___    ___   ___

---

5. Shade to show the fraction.

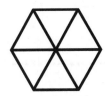 $\frac{3}{6}$ $\frac{2}{3}$ $\frac{4}{8}$

---

6. Label each number line with the correct fractions.

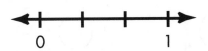   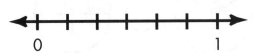

7. Show each fraction on the number line.

$\frac{6}{6}$

$\frac{2}{8}$

8. Write the equivalent fractions.

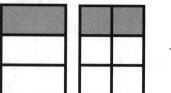 ⎯ = ⎯

9. Shade in the shapes to show each equivalent fraction. Then, write the equivalent fraction.

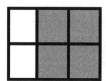 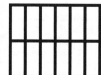 $\frac{4}{6} = $ ⎯

  $\frac{2}{4} = $ ⎯

10. Write the equivalent fractions.

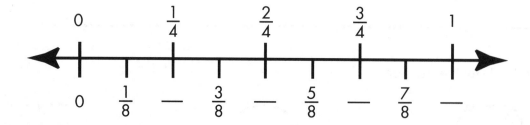

11. Compare using **<**, **>**, or **=**.

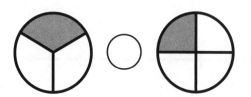

12. Compare using **<**, **>**, or **=**.

$\frac{1}{3}$ ◯ $\frac{3}{3}$ $\frac{4}{6}$ ◯ $\frac{1}{6}$

$\frac{1}{4}$ ◯ $\frac{3}{4}$ $\frac{1}{2}$ ◯ $\frac{2}{2}$

48

Name _____   Date _____

✦ Show What You Know ✦
Number and Operations — Fractions

1. How is the rectangle divided?

_____

2. Divide the square into thirds. Then, label each third with the appropriate fraction.

3. Write the fraction.

---

4. Write the fraction of the shaded parts.

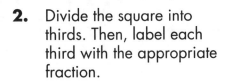

---

5. Shade to show the fraction.

 $\frac{1}{3}$  $\frac{2}{6}$  $\frac{3}{4}$

---

6. Label each number line with the correct fractions.

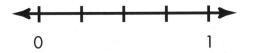 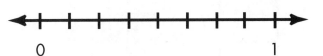

7. Show each fraction on the number line.

$\dfrac{7}{8}$

$\dfrac{3}{4}$

8. Write the equivalent fractions.

 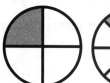 ____ = ____

---

9. Shade in the shapes to show each **equivalent** fraction. Then, write the equivalent fraction.

 $\dfrac{1}{3}$ = ____

 $\dfrac{1}{2}$ = ____

---

10. Complete the number line to show that $\dfrac{1}{3}$ and $\dfrac{2}{6}$ are equivalent.

---

11. Compare using **<**, **>**, or **=**.

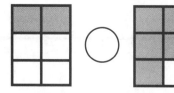

12. Compare using **<**, **>**, or **=**.

$\dfrac{1}{2} \bigcirc \dfrac{2}{3}$ $\dfrac{1}{6} \bigcirc \dfrac{2}{8}$

$\dfrac{2}{2} \bigcirc \dfrac{2}{4}$ $\dfrac{5}{6} \bigcirc \dfrac{4}{8}$

Identifying Fractions

Write the fraction of the shaded parts.

1.   ___

2.   ___

3.  ___

4.   ___

5.   ___

6.   ___

7.   ___

8. 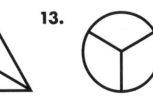 ___

9. 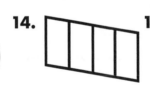 ___

10.   ___

Shade to show the fraction.

11.

$\dfrac{2}{6}$

12.

$\dfrac{1}{3}$

13.

$\dfrac{2}{3}$

14.

$\dfrac{1}{4}$

15.

$\dfrac{1}{3}$

16.

$\dfrac{2}{4}$

17.

$\dfrac{3}{6}$

18.

$\dfrac{5}{8}$

19.

1

20.

$\dfrac{1}{2}$

Name _____ Date _____

Identifying Fractions on a Number Line

Complete each number line. Then, show the fraction on the number line.

1. $\dfrac{1}{4}$	**2.** $\dfrac{3}{6}$
3. $\dfrac{5}{8}$	**4.** $\dfrac{2}{4}$
5. $\dfrac{2}{3}$	**6.** $\dfrac{3}{4}$
7. $\dfrac{1}{3}$	**8.** $\dfrac{1}{6}$
9. $\dfrac{3}{8}$ 	**10.** $\dfrac{4}{6}$

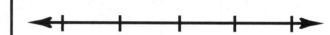
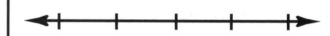

Fractions on a Number Line

Show each fraction on the number line.

1. $\dfrac{2}{6}$ ⟵───────────⟶	**2.** $\dfrac{2}{4}$ ⟵───────────⟶
3. $\dfrac{4}{4}$ ⟵───────────⟶	**4.** $\dfrac{2}{3}$ ⟵───────────⟶
5. $\dfrac{6}{8}$ ⟵───────────⟶	**6.** $\dfrac{5}{6}$ ⟵───────────⟶
7. $\dfrac{3}{6}$ ⟵───────────⟶	**8.** $\dfrac{3}{3}$ ⟵───────────⟶
9. $\dfrac{1}{8}$ ⟵───────────⟶	**10.** $\dfrac{3}{4}$ ⟵───────────⟶

Use these cards to have students match numeric fractions with the shaded model and/or number line. You may also choose to have students sort the cards into fraction families (halves, thirds, etc.). Or, have students draw a model or number line for a given fraction, or state the fraction for a given model or number line.

$\dfrac{1}{2}$ **A**	$\dfrac{1}{3}$ **B**	$\dfrac{2}{3}$ **C**
$\dfrac{1}{4}$ **D**	$\dfrac{2}{4}$ **E**	$\dfrac{3}{4}$ **F**
$\dfrac{4}{4}$ **G**	$\dfrac{1}{6}$ **H**	$\dfrac{2}{6}$ **I**

Fractions

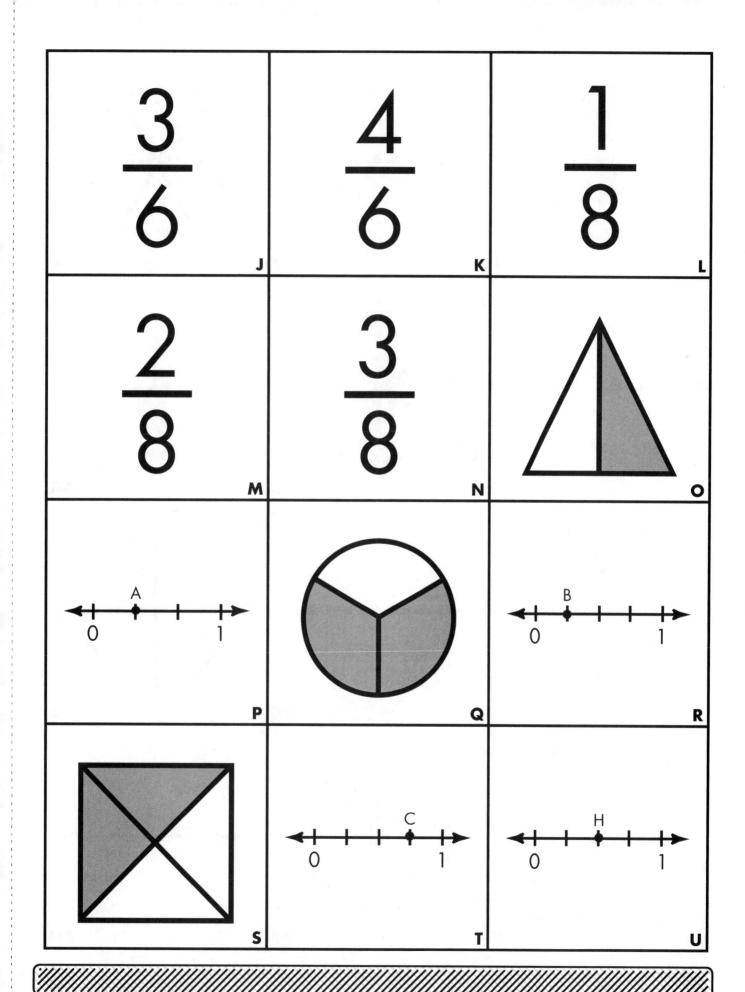

$$\frac{3}{6}$$

J

$$\frac{4}{6}$$

K

$$\frac{1}{8}$$

L

$$\frac{2}{8}$$

M

$$\frac{3}{8}$$

N

O

A

0   1

P

Q

B

0   1

R

S

C

0   1

T

H

0   1

U

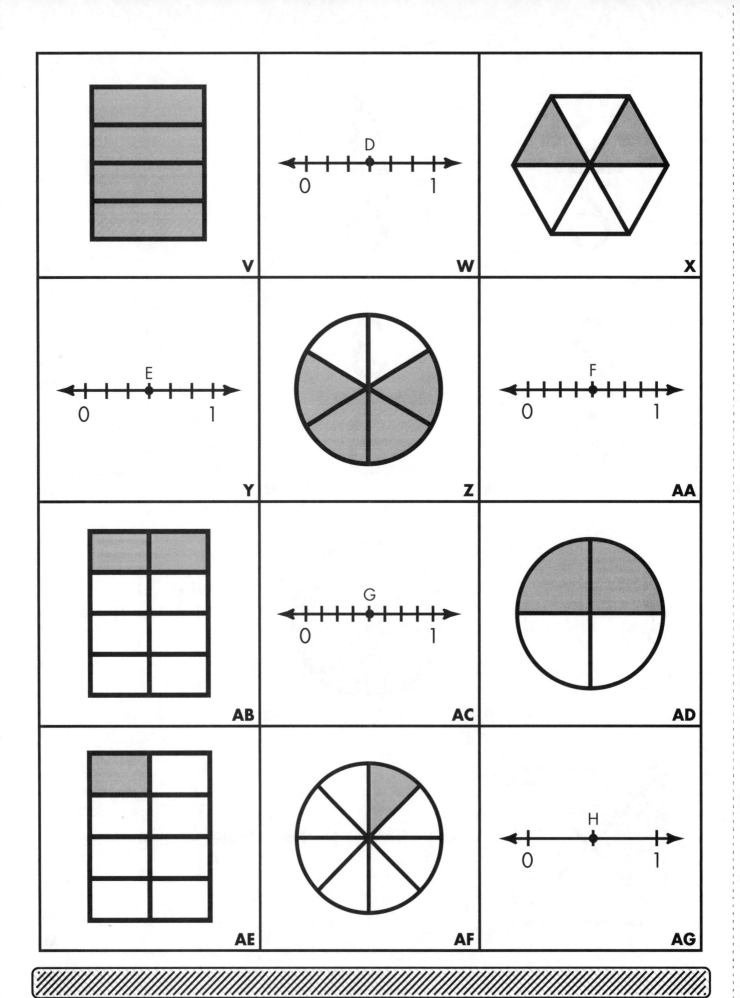

V

W

X

Y

Z

AA

AB

AC

AD

AE

AF

AG

Comparing Fractions

Identify each fraction. Circle the greater fraction.

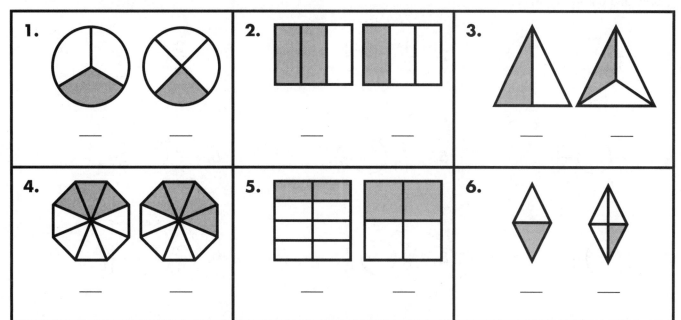

Shade the figure to match the fraction. Circle the greater fraction.

7.

$\frac{2}{3}$ $\frac{1}{3}$

8.

$\frac{1}{4}$ $\frac{2}{8}$

9.

$\frac{1}{2}$ $\frac{2}{3}$

10.

$\frac{3}{6}$ $\frac{5}{6}$

Comparing Fractions

Compare using **<**, **>**, or **=**.

1. $\frac{5}{10}$ ◯ $\frac{2}{10}$

2. $\frac{1}{3}$ ◯ $\frac{2}{3}$

3. $\frac{2}{3}$ ◯ $\frac{1}{2}$

4. $\frac{3}{10}$ ◯ $\frac{8}{10}$

5. $\frac{7}{10}$ ◯ $\frac{3}{5}$

6. $\frac{6}{7}$ ◯ $\frac{3}{7}$

7. $\frac{3}{8}$ ◯ $\frac{3}{4}$

8. $\frac{5}{9}$ ◯ $\frac{4}{9}$

9. $\frac{6}{11}$ ◯ $\frac{9}{11}$

10. $\frac{1}{5}$ ◯ $\frac{3}{5}$

11. $\frac{1}{3}$ ◯ $\frac{5}{8}$

12. $\frac{2}{3}$ ◯ $\frac{1}{3}$

13. $\frac{1}{2}$ ◯ $\frac{1}{4}$

14. $\frac{1}{3}$ ◯ $\frac{2}{3}$

15. $\frac{1}{5}$ ◯ $\frac{2}{10}$

16. $\frac{1}{4}$ ◯ $\frac{1}{3}$

17. $\frac{3}{4}$ ◯ $\frac{1}{2}$

18. $\frac{2}{3}$ ◯ $\frac{2}{9}$

19. $\frac{6}{10}$ ◯ $\frac{5}{10}$

20. $\frac{1}{5}$ ◯ $\frac{2}{5}$

21. $\frac{3}{4}$ ◯ $\frac{3}{8}$

22. Choose three problems from above. Draw a picture under each problem to explain the comparison.

Equivalent Fractions

Write each fraction. Then, draw lines to match the equivalent fractions.

1. 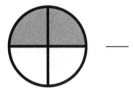 ___

2.  ___

3. 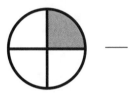 ___

4. 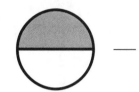 ___

5. 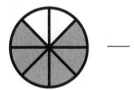 ___

6.  ___

7.  ___

8.  ___

Find each equivalent fraction.

9. $\frac{1}{2} = \frac{}{4}$	**10.** $\frac{2}{2} = \frac{3}{}$	**11.** $\frac{1}{3} = \frac{}{6}$	**12.** $\frac{4}{6} = \frac{2}{}$	**13.** $\frac{1}{3} = \frac{}{6}$
14. $\frac{3}{4} = \frac{}{8}$	**15.** $\frac{2}{3} = \frac{4}{}$	**16.** $\frac{4}{4} = \frac{2}{}$	**17.** $\frac{4}{8} = \frac{}{4}$	**18.** $\frac{1}{2} = \frac{3}{}$

19. Choose a set of equivalent fractions from problems 9–13. Draw a picture to show why they are equivalent.

20. Choose a set of equivalent fractions from problems 14–18. Use number lines to show why they are equivalent.

Equivalent Fractions on a Number Line

Use the number lines to answer the questions.

1. Are the fractions $\frac{1}{8}$ and $\frac{1}{4}$ equivalent? _____

Name two other fractions that are equivalent. _____ _____

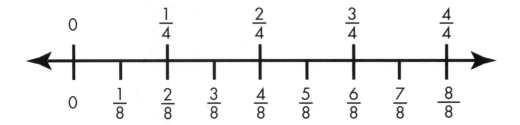

2. Are the fractions $\frac{1}{6}$ and $\frac{2}{3}$ equivalent? _____

Name two other fractions that are equivalent. _____ _____

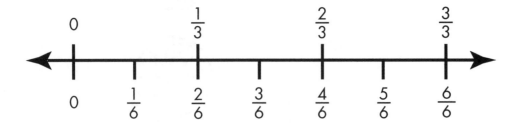

3. Are the fractions $\frac{3}{12}$ and $\frac{1}{4}$ equivalent? _____

Name two other fractions that are equivalent. _____ _____

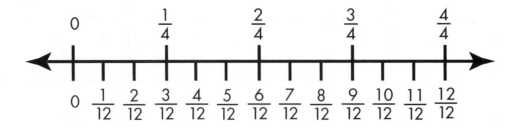

Write the fraction for the shape.

 ___

A

Complete the fraction.

 $= \dfrac{}{4}$

B

Complete the fraction.

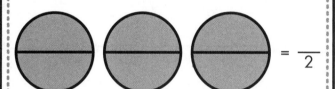 $= \dfrac{}{2}$

C

Write each fraction.

___   ___   ___

D

Shade the circle to show $\dfrac{7}{8}$.

E

Divide the square into halves. Label each half with the appropriate fraction.

F

Divide the circle into sixths. Then, shade the pieces to show $\dfrac{2}{6}$.

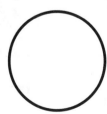

G

Draw a shape to represent each fraction.

$\dfrac{2}{3}$ $\dfrac{4}{6}$ $\dfrac{1}{8}$

H

Compare using **<**, **>**, or **=**.

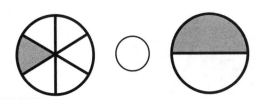

I

Compare using **<**, **>**, or **=**.

$\frac{1}{8}$ ◯ $\frac{1}{3}$ $\qquad$ $\frac{2}{8}$ ◯ $\frac{1}{2}$

$\frac{1}{6}$ ◯ $\frac{1}{4}$ $\qquad$ $\frac{1}{3}$ ◯ $\frac{1}{6}$

J

Label $\frac{2}{6}$ and $\frac{5}{6}$ on the number line.

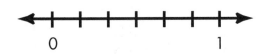

0 $\qquad$ 1

K

Divide the number line and label $\frac{1}{4}$ and $\frac{3}{4}$.

L

Are these two fractions equivalent? _____

How do you know? _____

_____

_____

M

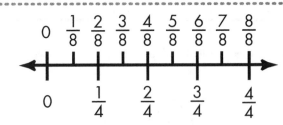

0 $\quad$ $\frac{1}{8}$ $\frac{2}{8}$ $\frac{3}{8}$ $\frac{4}{8}$ $\frac{5}{8}$ $\frac{6}{8}$ $\frac{7}{8}$ $\frac{8}{8}$

0 $\qquad$ $\frac{1}{4}$ $\qquad$ $\frac{2}{4}$ $\qquad$ $\frac{3}{4}$ $\qquad$ $\frac{4}{4}$

Are $\frac{2}{8}$ and $\frac{1}{4}$ equivalent? _____

Name two other fractions on the $\quad$ __ __
number line that are equivalent.

N

Draw a model of each fraction. Write the missing number to show equivalent fractions.

$$\frac{1}{3} = \frac{}{6}$$

O

The fractions $\frac{1}{2}$ and $\frac{4}{8}$ are equal.

true $\qquad$ **false**

P

Name _____ Date _____

Show What You Know
Measurement and Data

1. Solve.

Jaime packed 18 kilograms of apples equally into 3 bags. How many kilograms of apples were in each bag?

_____

2. Draw a pictograph for the data given. Then, answer the questions.

Favorite Pet	Number of Votes
Gerbils	4
Goldfish	3
Iguanas	1

Favorite Pet

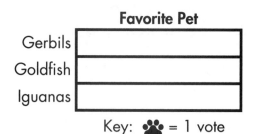

Key: 🐾 = 1 vote

What was the favorite pet? _____

What was the least favorite pet?

_____

How many people voted in all?

_____

3. Draw a bar graph for the data given. Then, answer the questions.

Desserts	Amount Sold
Cakes	25
Pies	19
Brownies	22

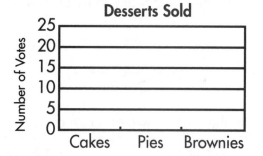

What dessert sold the least amount? _____

How many desserts were sold in all?

_____

How many more cakes than pies were sold?

_____

4. Find the area of each figure.

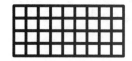 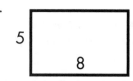 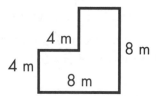

A = _____ A = _____ A = _____

5. Use the information to fill in the line plot.

$10\frac{1}{4}$ inches = 3 snakes

$10\frac{2}{4}$ inches = 8 snakes

$11\frac{1}{4}$ inches = 1 snake

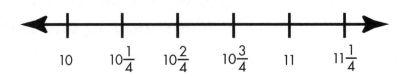

Lengths of Snakes at the Zoo (in.)

6. Find the area and perimeter of each figure.

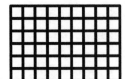

A = _____

P = _____

7

7

A = _____

P = _____

7. Solve.

Judd is painting an accent wall in his bedroom. The wall is 9 feet tall and 13 feet wide. If one gallon of paint covers 100 square feet of wall space, will one gallon be enough for Judd to paint the entire wall? Why or why not?

_____

_____

8. Write the time shown on each clock.

_____   _____   _____   _____

9. Use a time line to solve the problem.

Wendy arrives at work at 5:15 every morning. She leaves for a break at 8:25. She goes back to work at 2:45 and works until 6:00. How long is Wendy at work each day?

_____

Name _____ Date _____

✦ Show What You Know ✦
Measurement and Data

1. Solve.

Jessica bought 4 pounds of strawberries, 6 pounds of grapes, and 7 pounds of oranges to make a fruit salad. How many pounds of fruit did Jessica buy altogether?

_____

2. Draw a pictograph for the data given. Then, answer the questions.

Animals on the Farm	Amount
Chickens	40
Goats	15
Pigs	20

Animals on the Farm

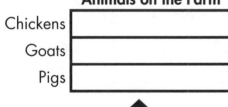

Chickens
Goats
Pigs

Key: 🏠 = 10

How many goats, chickens and pigs live on the farm? _____

How many more chickens than goats live on the farm? _____

If a chicken coop can hold 100 chickens, how many more chickens can the farmer have? _____

3. Draw a bar graph for the data given. Then, answer the questions.

Colors of Houses	Number of Houses
Blue	5
Yellow	10
Green	8

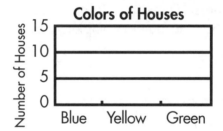

Which color house occurs most often in the neighborhood? _____

How many more houses are green than blue? _____

The neighborhood wants more equality when it comes to the color of the houses. What color should the next house be painted to help reach that goal?

_____

4. Find the area of each figure.

A = _____   A = _____   A = _____

5. Use the information to fill in the line plot.

$1\frac{1}{4}$ centimeters = 2 beetles

$1\frac{2}{4}$ centimeters = 1 beetles

$2\frac{1}{4}$ centimeters = 4 beetles

$$\xleftarrow{\quad} \; | \qquad | \qquad | \qquad | \qquad | \qquad | \; \xrightarrow{\quad}$$

1     $1\frac{1}{4}$ $1\frac{2}{4}$ $1\frac{3}{4}$ 2 $2\frac{1}{4}$

Lengths of Beetles in a Jar (cm)

6. Find the area and perimeter of each figure.

5

9

A = _____

P = _____

3 km   10 km

9 km

5 km   3 km

5 km

3 km

10 km

A = _____

P = _____

7. Solve.

Leigh is putting border up in her daughter's bedroom. The room is shaped like a rectangle and measures 10 feet by 12 feet. One roll of border paper is 25 feet long. How many rolls will Leigh have to buy to completely border her daughter's room? Explain.

_____

_____

8. Write the time shown on each clock.

_____   _____   _____   _____

9. Use a time line to solve the problem.

Norris parks at 7:34. He only has two quarters to put in the parking meter, which will pay for 30 minutes each. What time should he be back at his car?

_____

Volume and Mass
Word Problems

1. Mrs. Rinaldi filled a bucket to mop the floor. Does her bucket most likely hold 12 milliliters or 12 liters of water?

2. A school bus weighs about 15 tons. Mrs. Vasquez's car weighs 2 tons. How much do a school bus and Mrs. Vasquez's car weigh altogether?

3. Emily's bag of fruit weighs 32 ounces. Jason's bag of fruit weights 14 ounces. How many ounces do Emily's and Jason's bags weigh altogether?

4. A carton contains 2 liters of water. If there are 18 cartons of water, how many liters of water are there in all?

5. Luke's dog's water dish had 250 milliliters of water. His dog drank 104 milliliters. Then, his dad added 58 milliliters. How many milliliters of water does the dog's dish have now?

6. Ashley's little brother weighs 25 pounds. Crystal's little sister weighs 28 pounds. How many more pounds does Crystal's sister weigh than Ashley's brother?

Picture Graphs

Complete the bar graph for each set of data. Then, use the graph to answer the questions.

1.

Flower	Number in Garden
Daisies	6
Roses	10
Sunflowers	5
Lilies	4

Flowers In My Garden

Daisies	
Roses	
Sunflowers	
Lilies	

Key: ❀ = 2 flowers

2. How many total flowers are in the garden? _____

3. How many more roses are there than lilies? _____

4. How many daisies and sunflowers are there altogether? _____

5. Which flower occurs most often? _____

6.

Team	Miles
Team 1	60
Team 2	40
Team 3	140
Team 4	30

Miles Canoed

Team 1	
Team 2	
Team 3	
Team 4	

Key: ● = 20 miles

7. How many more miles did Team 3 travel than Team 2? _____

8. How many total miles did Team 1 and Team 4 canoe? _____

9. The lake is 100 miles long. Which team traveled more than the entire length of the lake?

_____

10. How many total miles did all four teams travel? _____

Name _____ Date _____

Bar Graphs

Complete the bar graph for each set of data. Then, use the graph to answer the questions.

1.

Month	Number of Students
January	30
April	60
July	70
October	20

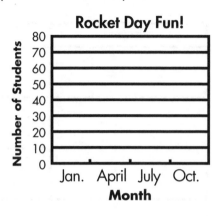

Rocket Day Fun!

2. Which month had the greatest attendance at Rocket Day? _____

3. How many more students attended Rocket Day in January than in October? _____

4. What was the total number of students that attended Rocket Day in all? _____

5. What was the combined attendance for both January and April? _____

6.

Food Item	Number Sold
Nachos	20
Hamburgers	50
Pretzels	50
Fries	30
Fruit bowls	70
Cotton candy	40

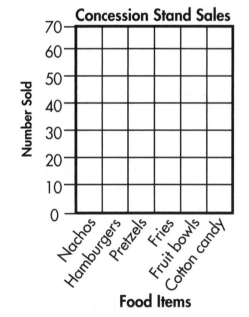

Concession Stand Sales

7. Which two items sold the least? _____

8. How many more hamburgers were sold than nachos? _____

9. Which item was sold the most? _____

10. Which item sold more—fries or cotton candy? _____

Creating Line Plots

1. Use a ruler to measure 10 items to the nearest $\frac{1}{2}$ inch. Record your data on the table.

Item	Length	Item	Length

2. Use the data from the table to make a line plot.

Finding Area

Find the area of each figure.

1.

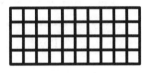

A = _____

2.

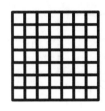

A = _____

3.

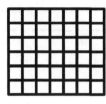

A = _____

4.

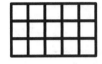

A = _____

5.

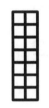

A = _____

6.

A = _____

7.

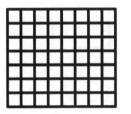

A = _____

8.

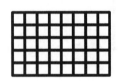

A = _____

9.

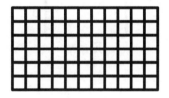

A = _____

10.

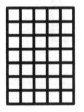

A = _____

11.

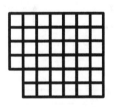

A = _____

12.

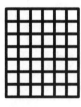

A = _____

13.

A = _____

14.

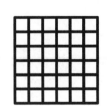

A = _____

15.

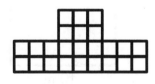

A = _____

Name _____ Date _____

Finding Area

Find the area of each figure.

1. 3 ft.
10 ft.

A = _____

2. 2 in.
2 in.

A = _____

3. 4 cm
6 cm

A = _____

4. 8 m
8 m

A = _____

5. 5 mm
9 mm

A = _____

6. 2 yd.
11 yd.

A = _____

7. 6 cm
7 cm

A = _____

8. 6 ft.
10 ft.

A = _____

9. 4 in.
4 in.

A = _____

10. 3 yd.
4 yd.

A = _____

11. 2 yd.
6 yd.

A = _____

12. 7 m
7 m

A = _____

13. 9 m
10 m

A = _____

14. 8 cm
12 cm

A = _____

15. 5 in.
8 in.

A = _____

Finding Area

Find the area of each figure. All measurements are in centimeters.

1.

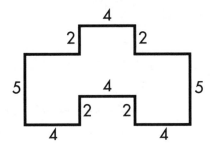

A = _____

2.

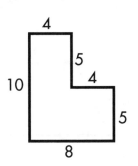

A = _____

3.

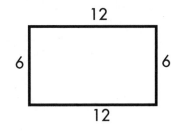

A = _____

4.

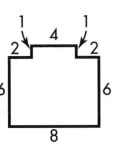

A = _____

5.

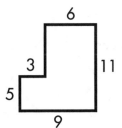

A = _____

6.

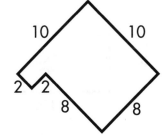

A = _____

7.

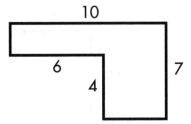

A = _____

8.

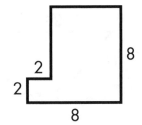

A = _____

9.

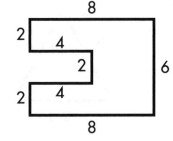

A = _____

10.

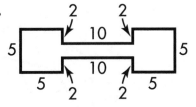

A = _____

11.

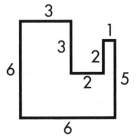

A = _____

12.

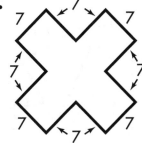

A = _____

Finding Perimeter

Find the perimeter of each figure.

1.

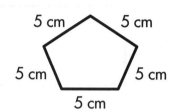

P = _____

2.

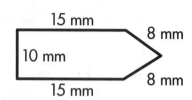

P = _____

3.

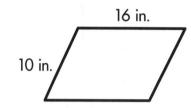

P = _____

4.

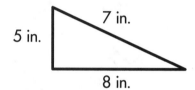

P = _____

5.

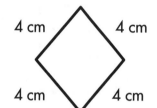

P = _____

6.

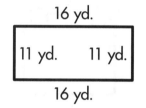

P = _____

7.

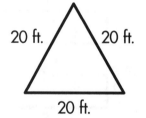

P = _____

8.

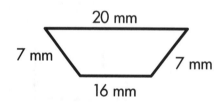

P = _____

9.

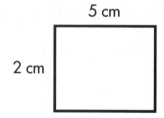

P = _____

10.

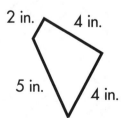

P = _____

11.

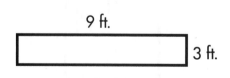

P = _____

12.

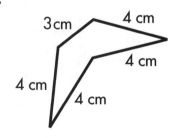

P = _____

Present a student with an area and perimeter card to assess their proficiency with finding area and perimeter of rectilinear figures. Or, choose several to create a whole-class assessment. You can have students find the area and/or perimeter of each figure, or compare the areas or perimeters of two or more figures (be sure to choose figures with the same unit or with units within the same measurement system). If desired, laminate the cards so that students can use write-on/wipe away markers to mark directly on each figure.

5 in. 3 in. **A**	4 m 4 m **B**	8 ft. 2 ft. **C**
7 km 7 km **D**	9 in. 5 in. **E**	10 cm 3 cm **F**
10 yd. 7 yd. **G**	20 mm 4 mm **H**	12 mi. 12 mi. **I**

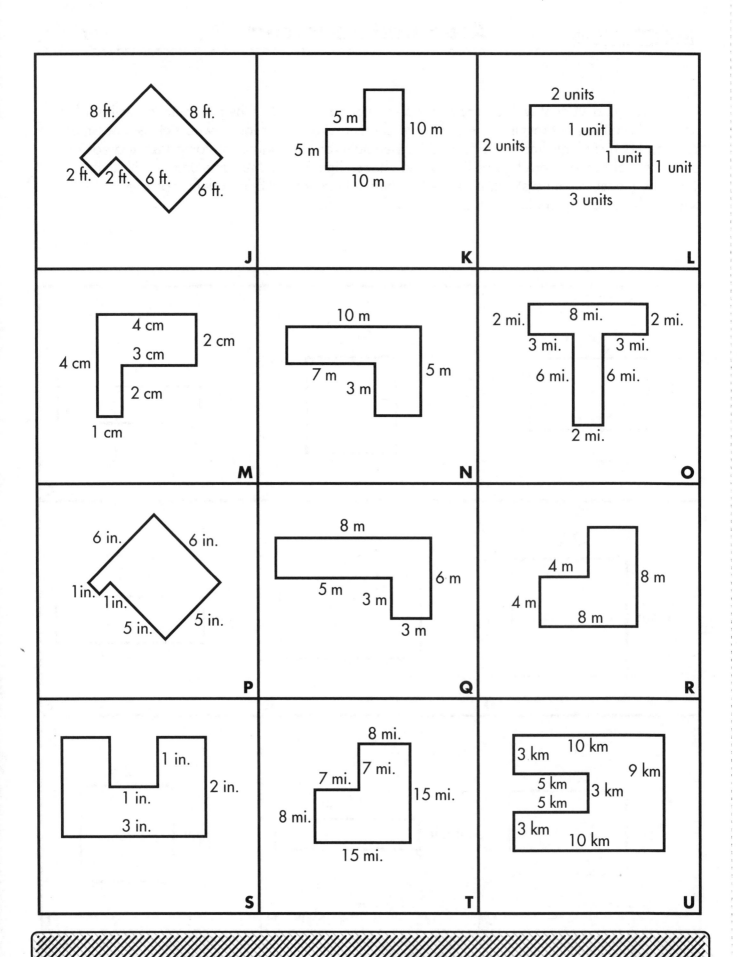

J

K

L

M

N

O

P

Q

R

S

T

U

Name _____ Date _____

Area and Perimeter Word Problems

Solve.

1. A square tile has sides that are 17 inches long. What is the perimeter?

2. Adam got a new puppy and needs to build a fence around the perimeter of his backyard. His backyard is rectangular. One side is 30 meters wide, and another side is 50 meters long. How many meters of fencing does he need?

3. The Murphy's property is very large and square shaped. Each edge of the property measures 6 kilometers long. What is the area of the Murphy's property?

4. The Underwood brothers are painting a wall in their living room. The wall measures 9 feet by 12 feet. What is the area of the wall?

5. Mr. Dolby wants to tile his kitchen floor. How many 1-foot square tiles will he need if his floor is 11 feet long by 9 feet wide?

6. A hexagon has sides that are all 7 millimeters long. What is the perimeter?

Name _____   Date _____

Elapsed Time

Use the clocks to help you find elapsed time.

1. Ashton rode his bike from 3:00 to 3:58. How long did he ride his bike?

  _____

2. Dave's game started at 1:00. It ended at 2:43. How long did the game last?

  _____

3. Casey's favorite movie starts at 8:15. It will last for 2 hours and 18 minutes. What time will the movie end?

 _____

4. Ian's cat wandered off at 4:12. Ian found him at 5:26. How long was his cat lost?

 _____

Read each problem. Use the number line to help you find elapsed time.

5. Brandy arrived at the bookstore at 4:15 pm. She left the bookstore at 8:10 pm. How long was Brandy at the bookstore?

 _____

6. Timothy arrived at work at 6:45 am. He left work to go home at 4:15 pm. How much time did Timothy spend at work?

 _____

7. Trisha leaves the house at 5:30 am. She goes to the lake and a friend's house, and gets home at 11:40 am. How long was Trisha out of the house?

 _____

8. Richard goes to school at 7:20 am. The last bell rings at 2:25 pm. How long is Richard in school?

 _____

9. The time is 3:43 pm. Dinner is at 5:45 pm. How long is it until dinner?

 _____

10. The video is 59 minutes long. We started watching it at 8:22 pm. What time will the video be over?

_____

Time

Present a student with a time card to assess their proficiency with telling and writing time to the nearest minute. Students can read each time or find the elapsed time between two cards. Students can also use two card clocks to create a word problem to solve. If desired, laminate the cards to make them more durable.

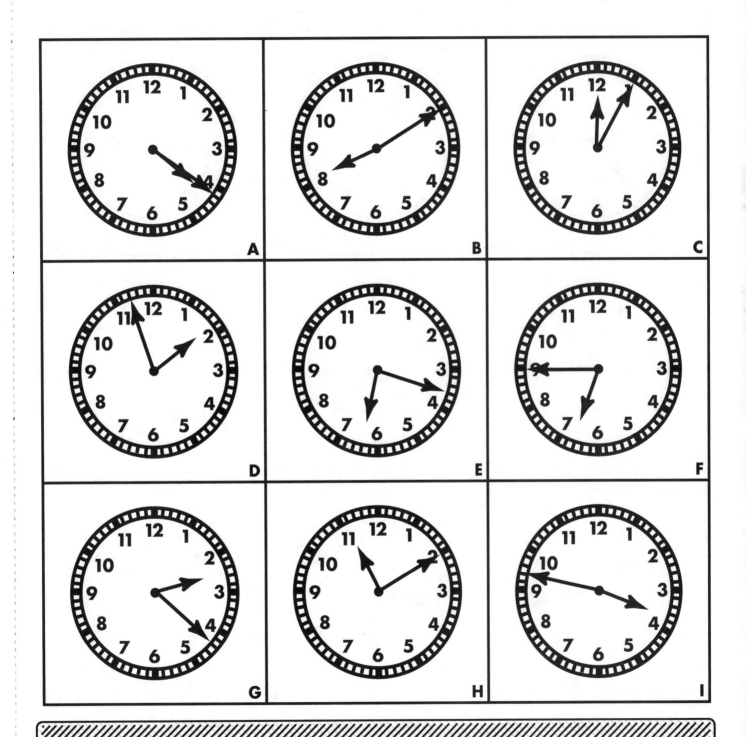

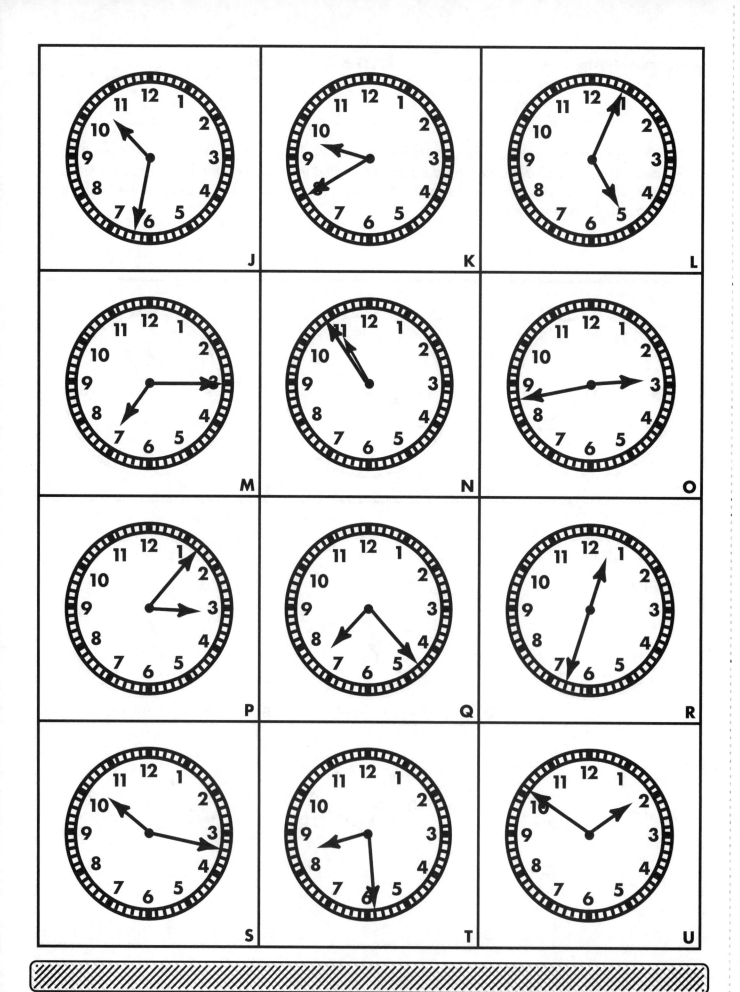

Solve.

A party hat has a mass of 30 grams. What is the mass of a set of 8 party hats?

A

Solve.

An adult weights about 63 kilograms. A female adult moose weighs about 396 kilograms. How much more does a moose weigh than a human?

B

Use the data given to draw a pictograph on the back of this ticket.

Classroom	Flowers Planted
Room A	45
Room B	20
Room C	25

C

Use the data given to draw a bar graph on the back of this ticket.

Plant Food	Growth (cm)
A	5
B	12
C	16
D	5
E	8

D

Use a ruler to measure 10 pencils or crayons to the nearest $\frac{1}{4}$ inch. Record each length below. Use the data to make a line plot on the back of this ticket.

E

Find the area of the figure.

A = _____

F

Find the area of the figure.

A = _____

G

Find the area of the figure.

5 yd.

3 yd.

A = _____

H

Find the area and perimeter of the figure.

6 ft.

6 ft.

A = _____ P = _____

I

Find the area and perimeter of the figure.

6 in.

2 in.

A = _____ P = _____

J

Find the area and perimeter of the figure.

5 cm

4 cm

A = _____ P = _____

K

Solve.

Rossi Elementary School must put new carpeting in all of the third-grade classrooms. There are 4 third-grade classrooms and each room is 10 yards by 12 yards. How much carpet does the school need to buy?

L

Solve.

Erica is carpeting her bedroom. Her bedroom measures 8 feet by 7 feet. The carpeting Erica wants to purchase costs $2 per square foot. How much money will Erica have to spend on carpet?

M

What time is it?

_____

N

Use the time line to find the elapsed time.

Bill left his house to go to the gym at 6:15. He came back from the gym at 8:52. How long was Bill gone?

6:15   8:52

⟵━┼━━━━━━━━┼━⟶ _____

O

Use a time line to find the elapsed time.

Austin lay down in his bed at 7:33. He could not fall asleep. He finally got up at 10:23 and went downstairs to watch TV. How long did Austin lay in his bed?

P

Name _____ Date _____

✦ Show What You Know ✦
Geometry

1. Name each polygon.

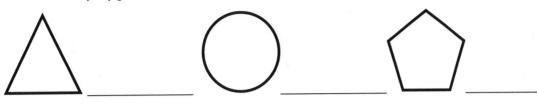

_____   _____   _____

2. Name each quadrilateral.

_____   _____   _____

3. Tell how many sides each figure has.

hexagon _____   octagon _____   trapezoid _____   triangle _____

4. Circle all of the parallelograms.

5. Divide each shape into the given amount of equal parts. Then, label each part with the appropriate fraction.

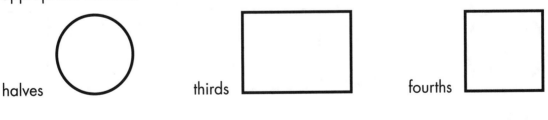

halves   thirds   fourths

fourths   halves   thirds

Name _____   Date _____

✦ Show What You Know ✦
Geometry

1. Name each quadrilateral.

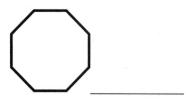 _____   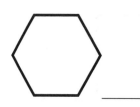 _____   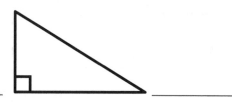 _____

2. Name each polygon.

 _____    _____   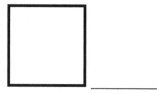 _____

3. Tell how many vertices each figure has.

rectangle _____   circle _____   pentagon _____   parallelogram _____

4. Circle all of the quadrilaterals.

       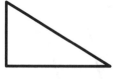 

5. Divide each shape into the given amount of equal parts. Then, label each part with the appropriate fraction.

thirds   fourths    halves

fourths   halves    fifths

Categorizing Shapes

Present a student with a polygon card to assess their proficiency with recognizing and classifying various polygons. Give a student a card and have him identify the polygon's attributes, such as name, number of sides and vertices, etc. You may also have him classify the shapes by number of sides and/or which ones have equal and opposite sides. If desired, laminate the cards for durability.

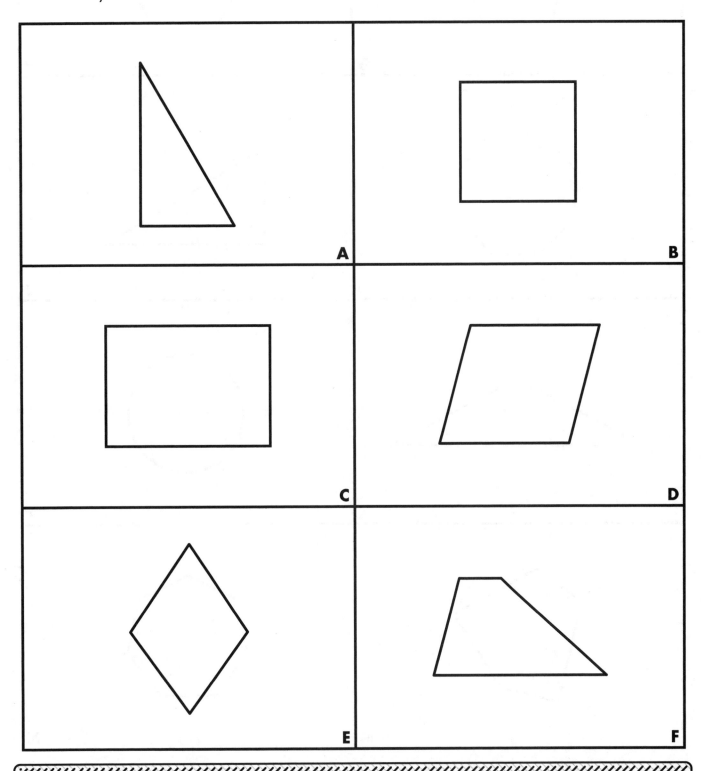

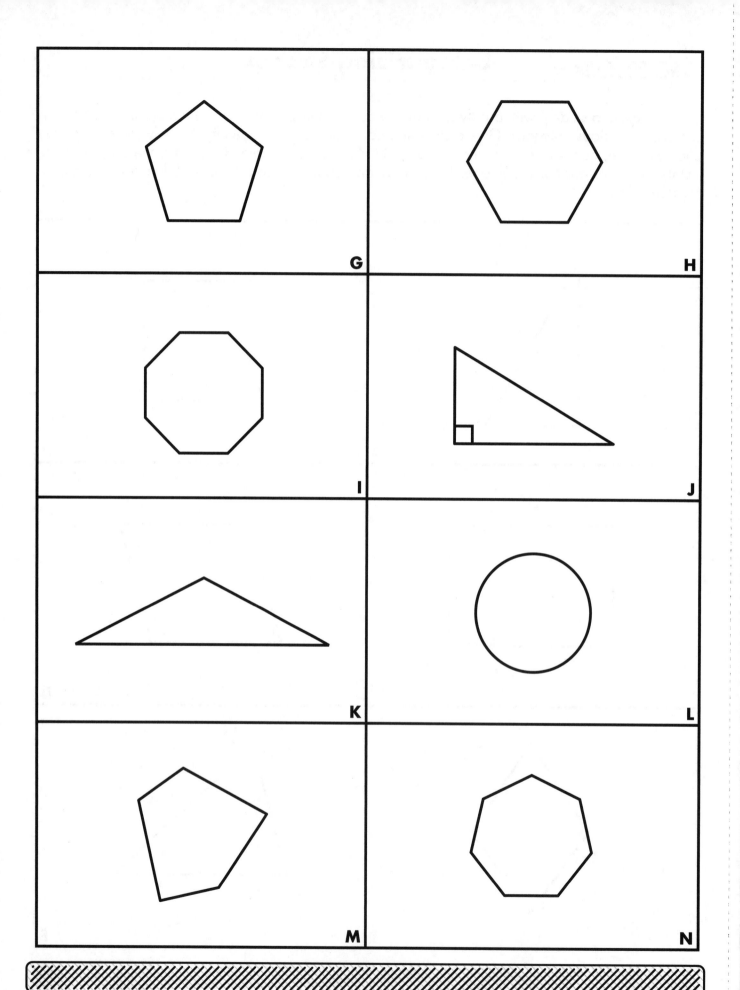

G

H

I

J

K

L

M

N

Name _____   Date _____

Partitioning Shapes

Tell how each shape is partitioned.

1.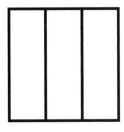

_____

2.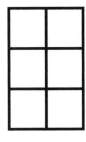

_____

3.

_____

Partition each shape into two, four, and six equal areas. Tell the fraction of each part.

	Two	Four	Six
4.	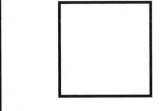 —	 —	—
5.	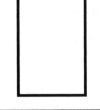 —	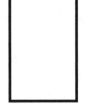 —	—
6.	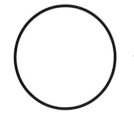 —	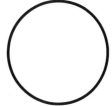 —	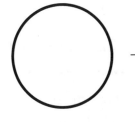 —
7.	 —	 —	—

Name _____ Date _____

Partitioning Shapes

Draw three different quadrilaterals. Partition at least one shape into 4 equal parts.

1.

2.

3.

4. The parts are all _____ .

Draw three different pentagons. Partition at least one shape into 2 equal parts.

5.

6.

7.

8. The parts are all _____ .

Draw three different hexagons. Partition at least one shape into 3 equal parts.

9.

10.

11.

12. The parts are all _____ .

Draw three different octagons. Partition at least one shape into 8 equal parts.

13.

14.

15.

16. The parts are all _____ .

A. Name each shape. Tell how they are similar and different.

_____   _____

_____

_____

B. What is the name of this shape? Are there other types of this shape? If so, draw them.

_____

C. Complete the attributes.

Number of Sides: ___   Number of Sides:___

Name: _____   Name: _____

D. Identify each polygon.

_____   _____

E. Draw each figure.

trapezoid   parallelogram

F. Draw three examples of a quadrilateral.

G. Draw three examples of a pentagon.

H. Solve. Draw a picture to help you.

Travis is going to mow his backyard. Each side of his yard is 10 feet long. The total distance around the yard is 50 feet. What shape is his yard?

Solve.

The flower bed in Natalie's yard is rectangular. The perimeter is 18 feet. If one side is 3 feet long, draw a picture of what the flower bed looks like. Include all of the dimensions.

I

Find at least three examples of each polygon around your classroom. Write the name of each object in the correct section.

Triangle	**Rectangle**

J

Tell how each shape is partitioned.

_____   _____

K

Tell how each shape is partitioned.

_____   _____

L

Partition each shape into halves. Tell the fraction of each part.

___   ___

M

Partition each shape into fourths. Tell the fraction of each part.

___   ___

N

Complete each statement with the words **All**, **Some**, **No**, or **None**.

_____ rectangles have 4 vertices.

_____ rectangles are parallelograms.

_____ rectangles are circles.

O

Complete each statement with the words **All**, **Some**, **No**, or **None**.

_____ triangles have 4 vertices.

_____ triangles are quadrilaterals.

_____ triangles have 3 vertices.

P

Answer Key

Pages 11–12
1. 4 × 3 = 12; 2. Check students' work.
3. 14, 12, 16; 4. 9, 14; 5. 8 ÷ 2 = 4; 6.
Check students' work. 5, 8; 7. 9, 5, 4; 8. 6, 6;
9. 8, 5; 10. 12, 84; 11. Answers will vary but
may include 6 × 5 = 30, 8 × 5 = 40,
63 ÷ 9 = 7, 24 ÷ 8 = 3; 12. 63 flowers;
13. 6 times; 14. 6 candies; 15. 9 people;
16. $33; 17. 61 cards

Pages 13–14
1. 6 × 3 = 18; 2. Check students' work.
3. 12, 9, 24; 4. 10, 3; 5. 12 ÷ 3 = 4; 6.
Check students' work. 3, 3; 7. 4, 8, 2; 8. 9,
56; 9. 7, 4; 10. 48, 28; 11. Answers will vary
but may include 36 ÷ 4 = 9, 35 ÷ 5 = 7,
4 × 7 = 28, and 6 × 4 = 24. 12. 35 marbles;
13. 96 books; 14. 7 goldfish; 15. 4 bracelets;
16. 30 gardens; 17. 67 poetry books

Page 15
1. Check students' work. 3 + 3 + 3 + 3 = 12,
3 × 4 = 12; 2. Check students' work.
3 + 3 + 3 + 3 + 3 = 15, 3 × 5 = 15; 3. Check
students' work. Factors: 1, 3, 5, 15, Factor
Pairs: 1, 15; 3, 5; 4. Check students' work.
Factors: 1, 2, 3, 4, 6, 8, 12, 24; Factor Pairs:
1, 24; 2, 12; 3, 8; 4, 6; 5–6. Check students'
work.

Page 16
1. 30, 14, 12, 16, 27, 55; 2. 70, 63, 40, 63,
10, 12; 3. 18, 9, 24, 49, 72, 20; 4. 72, 60,
22, 8, 21, 45; 5. 9, 8, 21, 20, 20, 32; 6. 54,
24, 28, 30, 28, 21; 7. 10, 16, 35, 48, 64,
99; 8. 4, 48, 72, 36, 6, 56; 9. 25, 18, 32,
24, 40, 81

Page 17
1. 27, 42, 20, 63, 48, 0; 2. 12, 40, 36, 0,
35, 18; 3. 5, 24, 16, 48, 0, 33; 4. 3, 60, 24,
18, 12, 18; 5. 24, 50, 18, 42, 81, 32; 6. 12,
48, 64, 27, 28, 0; 7. 49, 18, 24, 40, 40, 18;
8. 77, 24, 21, 6, 14, 15; 9. 90, 12, 25, 9, 8,
21

Page 18
1. Trent says 3. 2. Trent says 6. 3. Trent says
3. 4. Kayla says 8. 5. Kayla says 9. 6. Trent
says 2. 7. Kayla says 2. 8. Kayla says 2.
9. Kayla says 10. 10. Trent says 2. 11. Trent
says 4. 12. Kayla says 5. 13. Trent says 5.
14. Kayla says 6. 15. Trent says 2. 16. Kayla
says 120.

Page 19
1. 10 ÷ 2 = 5; 2. 16 ÷ 4 = 4; 3. 6; 4. 4;
5. Check students' work. 12 ÷ 3 = 4; 6. Check
students' work. 5 ÷ 1 = 5; 7. Check students'
work. 12 ÷ 4 = 3; 8. Check students' work.
18 ÷ 6 = 3

Page 20
1. 6, 9, 9, 4, 9, 1; 2. 8, 8, 3, 7, 4, 3; 3. 8, 9,
4, 7, 2, 4; 4. 5, 2, 8, 9, 8, 7; 5. 10, 7, 6, 9,
5, 7; 6. 3, 9, 2, 9, 4, 6; 7. 4, 3, 3, 2, 10, 1

Page 21
1. 5, 4, 3, 9, 3, 9; 2. 9, 8, 7, 1, 8, 7; 3. 4, 7,
9, 2, 2, 5; 4. 3, 3, 6, 5, 1, 9; 5. 3, 4, 9, 4, 6,
9; 6. 1, 8, 6, 9, 8, 6; 7. 5, 7, 6, 5, 3, 4

Answer Key

Page 22

1. Evan says 2. 2. Evan says 27. 3. Evan says 9. 4. Evan says 9. 5. Blair says 24. 6. Blair says 2. 7. Evan says 5. 8. Evan says 18. 9. Evan says 3. 10. Evan says 3. 11. Blair says 8. 12. Evan says 10. 13. Blair says 32. 14. Blair says 3. 15. Blair says 4. 16. Evan says 4.

Pages 23–26

A. 70 petals; B. 48 mi.; C. 60 eggs; D. 14 snails; E. 48 buckets; F. 9 animals; G. 20 stickers; H. 96 slices; I. 32 seeds; J. 30 spoons; K. 42 strawberries; L. 9 scoops; M. 35 bugs; N. 60 cents; O. 72 flowers; P. 15 short stories; Q. 24 peanuts; R. 20 flags; S. 3 papers; T. 6 cookies; U. 9 shells; V. 7 grapes; W. 6 dogs; X. 8 dolls; Y. 9 erasers; Z. 8 pencils; AA. 6 cakes; AB. 5 groups; AC. 7 types of bugs; AD. 6 bags; AE. 5 slices; AF. 2 water bottles; AG. 12 pairs of shoes; AH. 3 months; AI. 9 chairs; AJ. 6 books; AK. $9; AL. 22 horses

Pages 27–28

A. 13 balloons; B. 17 cans and boxes; C. 52 apples; D. $6; E. 3 times; F. 19 pages; G. 60 cents; H. 30 marbles; I. Yes, answers will vary. J. 345 beads; K. 59 shots; L. 49 letters, 14 vowels, 35 consonants; M. No, answers will vary but may include 30 more gumdrops are needed. N. 12 flowers

Page 29

1. 30 cents; 2. 10 swimmers; 3. 1 ball; 4. 81 computers; 5. 63 Gingersnap Delights; 6. 7 players

Page 30

1. 4, 4; 2. 3, 3; 3. 4, 4; 4. 5, 5; 5. 5, 5; 6. 3, 3; 7. 3, 3; 8. 6, 6; 9. 5, 5; 10. 9, 9; 11. 5, 5; 12. 2, 2; 13. 4, 4; 14. 2, 2; 15. 6, 6; 16. 8, 8; 17. 9, 9; 18. 11, 11

Pages 31–32

A. 6 $\times$ 4 = 24; B. Check students' work. C. 1. 20, 2. 18, 3. 14, 4. 54, 5. 30, 6. 24, 7. 16, 8. 24; D. 1. 9, 2. 8, 3. 5, 4. 8, 5. 4, 6. 12, 7. 9, 8. 5; E. 21 ÷ 3 = 7; F. Check studentsÔ work. 3, 9; G. 1. 7, 2. 6, 3. 7, 4. 3, 5. 11, 6. 8, 7. 4, 8. 4; H. Answers will vary but may include 1. 3 × 9 = 27, 2. 18 ÷ 2 = 9, 3. 50 ÷ 5 = 10, 4. 8 × 7 = 56; I. 66 cents; J. $6; K. 28 mi.; L. 7 pieces; M. 9 counters; N. 5 tables; O. 14 times; P. 211 insects

Pages 33–34

1. 532; 2. 182; 3. 1,089; 4. 256; 5. 158; 6. 1,133; 7. 193; 8. 783; 9. 1,382; 10. 268; 11. 474; 12. 384; 13. 276; 14. 582; 15. 281; 16. 184; 17. 882; 18. 187; 19. 1,324; 20. 395; 21. 24, 142, 120; 22. 70, 80, 50, 60, 20, 30, 60, 100; 23. 700, 400, 300, 200, 600, 900, 700, 100; 24. 403 empty seats; 25. 411 tickets; 26. 511 pairs; 27. 90, 160, 400, 540, 240, 160, 480

Answer Key

Pages 35–36
1. 1,633; 2. 1,609; 3. 1,272; 4. 389;
5. 357; 6. 106; 7. 279; 8. 298; 9. 1,060;
10. 1,007; 11. 278; 12. 958; 13. 1,314;
14. 837; 15. 96; 16. 644; 17. 1,085;
18. 641; 19. 208; 20. 781; 21. 44; 120;
120; 22. 60, 90, 60, 60, 30, 50, 70, 80;
23. 400, 900, 900, 700, 500, 800, 500,
100; 24. $348; 25. 1759; 26. $280; 27. 30,
60, 90, 200, 120, 120, 60

Page 37
1. 902; 2. 1,076; 3. 289; 4. 1,164; 5. 289;
6. 370; 7. 685; 8. 212; 9. 1,153; 10. 593;
11. 823; 12. 120; 13. 59; 14. 382;
15. 1,165; 16. 678; 17. 1,296; 18. 489;
19. 435; 20. 480; 21. 1,656; 22. 148;
23. 1,175; 24. 708; 25. 625; 26. 960;
27. 289; 28. 233; 29. 411; 30. 691

Page 38
1. 19; 2. 21; 3. 30; 4. 44; 5. 97; 6. 16;
7. 133; 8. 153; 9. 123; 10. 83; 11. 142;
12. 150; 13. 251; 14. 120; 15. 120;
16. 223; 17. 157; 18. 95; 19. 163;
20. 183; 21. 188; 22. 39; 23. 120; 24. 212;
25. 172; 26. 155; 27. 188; 28. 54; 29. 154;
30. 180; 31. 140; 32. 134; 33. 65; 34. 105;
35. 114; 36. 127

Page 39
1. 369; 2. 901; 3. 238; 4. 417; 5. 33;
6. 326; 7. 732; 8. 165; 9. 222; 10. 521;
11. 290; 12. 222; 13. 121; 14. 15;
15. 1,108; 16. 226; 17. 606; 18. 1,003;
19. 112; 20. 129; 21. 1,005; 22. 397;
23. 296; 24. 476

Page 40
1. 6,556, 2. 9,315; 3. 6,796; 4. 7,162;
5. 9,971; 6. 960; 7. 1,540; 8. 2,380;
9. 3,340; 10. 3,881; 11. 6,219; 12. 4,810;
13. 733; 14. 2,635; 15. 830; 16. 3,764;
17. 9,990; 18. 9,311; 19. 7,296; 20. 9,793;
21. 4,092; 22. 595; 23. 1,582; 24. 5,291;
25. 7,481; 26. 8,891; 27. 5,524; 28. 9,044;
29. 3,490; 30. 7,641

Pages 41–42
A. 62 flyers; B. 1,019 students; C. 1,361 tiles;
D. $383; E. 510 paper clips; F. 1,061 pennies;
G. 3,218 students; H. $22; I. 54 years old;
J. 886 pages; K. 112 in.; L. 134 years old;
M. 137 in.; N. 191 mi.

Page 43
1. 50, 100, 80, 30, 50; 2. 30, 70, 50, 20,
20; 3. 100, 10, 60, 50, 40; 4. 700, 300,
100, 800, 400; 5. 700, 200, 400, 500,
300; 6. 900, 500, 900, 800, 500; 7. 2,700,
8,040, 9,690, 3,300; 8. 2,800, 4,700,
3,900, 9,600; 9. 240, 290, 3,210, 2,600;
10. 5,670, 7,800, 4,200, 6,600

Page 44
1. 540; 2. 210; 3. 640; 4. 480; 5. 300;
6. 400; 7. 810; 8. 150; 9. 180; 10. 120;
11. 420; 12. 480; 13. 180; 14. 240;
15. 280; 16. 350; 17. 140; 18. 100;
19. 490; 20. 450

Answer Key

Pages 45–46
A. 212, 136, 1,218, 104, 29, 740; B. 49,
206, 124, 152; C. 170, 82, 42, 110;
D. Check student's work for opposite operation.
553, 909; E. 990, 3,222, 3,280, 5,720;
F. 4,995, 927, 2,025, 875; G. 97 pages;
H. 155 are not peanuts; I. 434 mi.; J. 36 dogs;
K. $271; L. 889 pages; M. 70, 70, 90, 90,
50, 70, 40, 80; N. 200, 500, 700, 200,
200, 900, 500, 900; O. 2,300, 900, 9,320,
1,900, 3,610, 2,900, 700, 500; P. 150, 100,
60, 300, 280, 320, 480, 120, 90, 180

Pages 47–48
1. thirds; 2. Check students' work. 3. $\frac{6}{8}$;
4. $\frac{1}{3}$, $\frac{2}{6}$, $\frac{3}{4}$; 5–7. Check students' work. 8. $\frac{1}{3}$ =
$\frac{2}{6}$; 9. Check students' work. $\frac{8}{12}$, $\frac{4}{8}$; 10. $\frac{2}{8}$, $\frac{4}{8}$,
$\frac{6}{8}$, $\frac{8}{8}$; 11. >; 12. <, >, <, <

Pages 49–50
1. sixths; 2. Check students' work. 3. $\frac{1}{2}$;
4. $\frac{3}{8}$, $\frac{2}{3}$, $\frac{4}{6}$; 5–7. Check students' work.
8. $\frac{1}{4}$ = $\frac{2}{8}$; 9. Check students' work. $\frac{2}{6}$, $\frac{4}{8}$;
10. Check studentsÔ work. 11. <; 12. <, <, >,
>

Page 51
1. $\frac{1}{4}$; 2. $\frac{3}{6}$; 3. $\frac{3}{4}$; 4. $\frac{2}{8}$; 5. $\frac{5}{6}$; 6. $\frac{4}{6}$; 7. $\frac{2}{3}$;
8. $\frac{1}{6}$; 9. $\frac{7}{8}$; 10. $\frac{2}{4}$; 11–20. Check students'
work.

Page 52
Check students' work.

Page 53
Check students' work.

Page 57
1. $\frac{1}{3}$, $\frac{1}{4}$; $\frac{1}{3}$ should be circled; 2. $\frac{2}{3}$, $\frac{1}{3}$; $\frac{2}{3}$
should be circled; 3. $\frac{1}{2}$, $\frac{1}{3}$; $\frac{1}{2}$ should be
circled; 4. $\frac{3}{8}$, $\frac{4}{8}$; $\frac{4}{8}$ should be circled; 5. $\frac{2}{8}$,
$\frac{2}{4}$; $\frac{2}{4}$ should be circled; 6. $\frac{1}{2}$, $\frac{1}{4}$; $\frac{1}{2}$ should be
circled; 7. Check students' work. $\frac{2}{3}$ should be
circled. 8. Check students' work. Both should
be circled. 9. Check students' work. $\frac{2}{3}$ should
be circled. 10. Check students' work. $\frac{5}{6}$ should
be circled.

Page 58
1. >; 2. <; 3. >; 4. <; 5. >; 6. >; 7. <; 8. >;
9. <; 10. <; 11. <; 12. >; 13. >; 14. <; 15. =;
16. <; 17. >; 18. >; 19. >; 20. <; 21. >;
22. Check students' work.

Page 59
1. $\frac{2}{4}$; 2. $\frac{4}{6}$; 3. $\frac{1}{4}$; 4. $\frac{1}{2}$; 5. $\frac{6}{8}$; 6. $\frac{3}{4}$; 7. $\frac{2}{3}$;
8. $\frac{2}{8}$; Matches: 1, 4; 3, 8; 5, 6; 7, 2; 9. 2;
10. 3; 11. 2; 12. 3; 13. 2; 14. 6; 15. 6;
16. 2; 17. 2; 18. 6; 19–20. Check students'
work.

Answer Key

Page 60

1. no, $\frac{1}{4}$ and $\frac{2}{8}$, $\frac{2}{4}$ and $\frac{4}{8}$, $\frac{3}{4}$ and $\frac{6}{8}$, $\frac{4}{4}$ and $\frac{8}{8}$; 2. no, $\frac{1}{3}$ and $\frac{2}{6}$, $\frac{2}{3}$ and $\frac{4}{6}$, $\frac{3}{3}$ and $\frac{6}{6}$; 3. yes, $\frac{2}{4}$ and $\frac{6}{12}$, $\frac{3}{4}$ and $\frac{9}{12}$, $\frac{4}{4}$ and $\frac{12}{12}$

Pages 61–62

A. $\frac{3}{4}$; B. 8; C. 6; D. $\frac{1}{6}$, $\frac{5}{8}$, $\frac{1}{2}$; E–H. Check students' work. I. <; J. <, <, <, >; K–L. Check students' work. M. yes, because equal amounts are shaded. N. yes, Answers will vary. O. Check students' work. 2; P. true

Pages 63–64

1. 6 kg; 2. Check students' work. gerbil, iguana, 8; 3. Check students' work. pies, 66, 6; 4. 36 sq. units, 40 sq. units, 48 sq. m; 5. Check students' work. 6. 54 sq. units, 30 units, 49 sq. units, 28 units; 7. No, he has to paint 117 square feet. 8. 3:17, 12:59, 6:30, 8:04; 9. 6 hr., 25 min.

Pages 65–66

1. 17 lb.; 2. Check students' work. 75, 25, 60; 3. Check students' work. yellow, 3, blue; 4. 15 sq. units, 16 sq. units, 17 sq. units; 5. Check students' work. 6. 45 sq. units, 28 units; 75 sq. km, 48 km; 7. 2 rolls, Answers will vary. 8. 2:19, 9:15, 10:55, 1:09; 9. 8:34

Page 67

1. 12 L; 2. 17 T; 3. 46 oz.; 4. 36 L; 5. 204 mL; 6. 3 lb.

Page 68

1. Check students' work. 2. 25; 3. 6; 4. 11; 5. roses; 6. Check students' work. 7. 100; 8. 90; 9. Team 3; 10. 270

Page 69

1. Check students' work. 2. July; 3. 10; 4. 180; 5. 90; 6. Check students' work. 7. nachos and fries; 8. 30; 9. fruit bowls; 10. cotton candy

Page 70

Check students' work.

Page 71

1. 15 sq. units; 2. 49 sq. units, 3. 42 sq. units; 4. 40 sq. units; 5. 14 sq. units; 6. 24 sq. units; 7. 56 sq. units; 8. 40 sq. units; 9. 66 sq. units; 10. 35 sq. units; 11. 40 sq. units; 12. 42 sq. units; 13. 26 sq. units; 14. 36 sq. units; 15. 24 sq. units

Page 72

1. 30 sq. ft.; 2. 4 sq. in.; 3. 24 sq. cm; 4. 64 sq. m; 5. 45 sq. mm; 6. 22 sq. yd.; 7. 42 sq. cm; 8. 60 sq. ft.; 9. 16 sq. in.; 10. 12 sq. yd.; 11. 12 sq. yd.; 12. 49 sq. m; 13. 90 sq. m; 14. 96 sq. cm; 15. 40 sq. in.

Page 73

1. 60 sq. cm; 2. 60 sq. cm; 3. 72 sq. cm; 4. 52 sq. cm; 5. 81 sq. cm; 6. 84 sq. cm; 7. 46 sq. cm; 8. 52 sq. cm; 9. 40 sq. cm; 10. 60 sq. cm; 11. 29 sq. cm; 12. 245 sq. cm

Page 74

1. 30 cm; 2. 52 in.; 3. 56 mm; 4. 20 in.; 5. 16 cm; 6. 54 yd.; 7. 60 ft.; 8. 50 mm; 9. 14 cm; 10. 15 in.; 11. 24 ft.; 12. 19 cm

Answer Key

Pages 75–76
A. 15 sq. in., 16 in.; B. 16 sq. m, 16 m;
C. 16 sq. ft., 20 ft.; D. 49 sq. km, 28 km;
E. 45 sq. in., 28 in.; F. 30 sq. cm, 26 cm;
G. 70 sq. yd., 34 yd.; H. 80 sq. mm, 48 mm;
I. 144 sq. mi., 48 mi.; J. 52 sq. ft., 32 ft.;
K. 75 sq. m, 40 m; L. 5 sq. units, 10 units;
M. 10 sq. cm, 16 cm; N. 29 sq. m, 30 m;
O. 28 sq. mi., 32 mi.; P. 31 sq. in., 24 in.;
Q. 33 sq. m, 28 m; R. 48 sq. m, 32 m;
S. 5 sq. in., 12 in.; T. 176 sq. mi., 60 mi.;
U. 75 sq. km, 48 km

Page 77
1. 68 in.; 2. 160 m; 3. 36 sq. km;
4. 108 sq. ft.; 5. 99 tiles; 6. 42 mm

Page 78
1. 58 min.; 2. 1 hr. 43 min.; 3. 10:33;
4. 1 hr. 14 min.; 5. 3 hr., 55 min.;
6. 9 hr., 30 min.; 7. 6 hr., 10 min.;
8. 7 hr., 5 min.; 9. 2 hr., 2 min.; 10. 9:21

Pages 79–80
A. 4:21; B. 8:10; C. 12:05; D. 2:57; E. 6:18;
F. 6:45; G. 2:22; H. 11:10; I. 3:47; J. 10:32;
K. 9:40; L. 5:04; M. 7:15; N. 10:54; O. 2:43;
P. 3:07; Q. 7:23; R. 12:33; S. 10:17; T. 8:29;
U. 1:51

Pages 81–82
A. 240 g; B. 333 kg; C–E. Check students'
work. F. 18 sq. units; G. 13 sq. units;
H. 15 sq. yd.; I. A = 36 sq. ft., P = 24 ft.;
J. A = 12 sq. in., P = 16 in.; K. A = 20 sq. cm;
P = 18 cm; L. 480 sq. yd.; M. $112;
N. 10:12; O. 2 hr. 37 min.

Page 83
1. triangle, circle, pentagon; 2. square,
rectangle, rhombus; 3. 6, 8, 4, 3; 4. Check
students' work. 5. Check students' work.

Page 84
1. trapezoid, parallelogram, square;
2. octagon, hexagon, triangle; 3. 4, 0, 5, 4;
4. Check students' work. 5. Check students'
work.

Page 87
1. thirds; 2. sixths; 3. fourths; 4–6. Check
students' work.

Page 88
1–3. Check students' work. 4. fourths;
5–7. Check students' work. 8. halves;
9–11. Check students' work. 12. thirds;
13–15. Check students' work. 16. eighths

Pages 89–90
A. rectangle and square, Answers will vary
but may include they are both quadrilaterals,
but the square has four equal sides, while the
rectangle has only opposite sides equal.
B. triangle, yes, Answers will vary but may
include there are acute, obtuse, and right
triangles, as well as equilateral, isosceles,
and scalene triangles. C. 8, octagon; 4,
parallelogram; D. quadrilateral, triangle;
E–G. Check students' work. H. pentagon;
I–J. Check students' work. K. halves, fourths;
L. thirds, eighths; M–N. Check students' work.
O. All, All, No; P. No, No, All